Syrian or Golden Hamsters Owners Guide

Facts and information all about Syrian hamsters including care, food, diet, cages, pregnancy, breeding, behavior, toys, wheels, lifespan

Lyndsey McMahon

Published by Planet Gyrus Publication, Sunderland UK
Publisher Contact: publishing@planetgyrus.com

ISBN 978-0-9926334-0-0

Disclaimer: At the writing of this book, due diligence was done to
ensure accurate and up to date information regarding hamster
ownership and care. Information in this book is intended for
personal use of the reader only. The information is not intended to
replace professional advice. Reader reads and utilizes all information
in this book at their discretion and assumes full responsibility for
the utilization and result of information. Author and associates, and
publisher and associates assume no responsibility for any injuries,
losses, and/or any other damages that may result from the use of
the information in this book.

Acknowledgements

Special thanks to my husband Ian for being a supportive husband during the time it took me to write this book. I could not have written it without his willingness to pick up the slack and do more than his fair share during my hours at the computer. I am grateful for all of his help and understanding.

Thanks to Holly and Lily, my beautiful daughters and inspiration for writing this book.

Contents

ABOUT THE AUTHOR 8

INTRODUCTION 10

1: Meet the Syrian Hamster 12

A Brief History of the Syrian Hamster 12

2: A Close-Up View of the Syrian Hamster 16

Syrian Hamster Coats... 17

Longhaired or Shorthaired 17

Satin Coat 17

Rex Coat 17

Syrian Coat Patterns.. 17

Banded... 18

Dominant Spotted 18

Roan 18

Tortoise Shell.. 19

Coat Colors... 19

Hamster Size and Characteristics... 20

The Syrian Hamster's Body.. 21

Hamsters Make Great Pets... 23

Considerations before Shopping for a Hamster.................... 26

3: The Longhaired Syrian Hamster.. 28

4: Choose Your Syrian Hamster.. 32

Where to Shop for a Hamster 33

Tips for Buying a Healthy, Happy Hamster.............................. 34

Check the Hamster's Health.. 34

How much does a Hamster Cost? 37

Have a Safe Trip Home 38

5: Make Your Hamster Feel at Home................................... 40

The Cage... 41

Where Will You Place Your Hamster Home? 52

Cleaning Your Hamster's Home 54

6: What Do Hamsters Eat? 56

7: Keep Your Hamster Safe 66

How to Safely Handle Your Hamster................................. 66

Keep Your Escape Artist Safe... 69

8: Understanding Your Hamster's Body Language 72

9: Hamster Health... 76

Characteristics of a Healthy Hamster 77

The Dreaded Wet Tail Disease... 78

Deficiency Syndrome 79

Meningitis (LCM: Lymphocytic Chorio-Meningitis) 79

A Trip to the Vet.. 81

Symptoms, Probable Cause, and Possible Remedy 82

10: Hamster Hygiene and Health 86

11: Breeding Your Syrian Hamster 92

Helpful Breeding Tips.. 97

12: The Pregnant Syrian Hamster and Her Pups 100

Take Care of Mommy Hamster... 101

The Birth of the Pups 103

The Pups 108

13: Syrian Hamster Tidbits... 112

Did You Know that Hamsters Can Go Dormant? 113

Did You Know that Your Hamster is Intelligent? 113

Did You Know… ? 114

14: Quick Tip References 118

Shopping for a Hamster 118

Hamster Habitat 119

Hamster Health 119

Keep Good Health Records 121

Hamsters and Medicine 123

ABOUT THE AUTHOR

Author Lyndsey McMahon and her daughters joined the millions of other people who wanted to have hamsters for pets. Lyndsey felt it would help teach her young daughters, Holly and Lily, the responsibility of caring for a living animal, and provide them with a fun experience.

It was also important to Lyndsey that her daughters have plenty of information and understand how to take the best care of their hamster. So, she did what any good writer and mom would do— she researched the topic and wrote a book on it!

In researching the book, Lyndsey found that hamsters make wonderful little pets, and her daughters were happy to confirm her research!

INTRODUCTION

Hamsters are fascinating creatures that can bring hours of entertainment and fun to anyone's life. From the way they stand on their back legs and gnaw away at a tiny sliver of food while staring you down, to the way they sit perfectly still and then suddenly scamper across their cage, to the way they perform tricks in their hamster ball, they bring smiles to our faces. It is incredible that something so small could have such a big personality.

Even though they are tiny animals, compared to many other common household pets, hamsters have specific needs for housing, food, care, and good health. They have been studied and observed as pets for long enough now for us to understand their habits, health concerns, and daily needs. This book is a guide for just that purpose. This guide will help you understand hamsters so you can take the best care of your hamster.

© Puchikumo / Klara S Fotolia

1: Meet the Syrian Hamster

The friendly little creatures in the photo above are Adar, which means ruler or prince in his native land of Syria, and Annie. Adar and Annie are the subjects of this fun, easy to follow guide that will tell you everything you need to know about their kind, Syrian Hamsters, also commonly known as golden hamsters or teddy bear hamsters. In this guide, the names Syrian hamster, golden hamster, and teddy bear hamster are interchangeable, but for the sake of simplicity, the name Syrian hamster will be used.

A Brief History of the Syrian Hamster

So, exactly who is this chubby-cheeked little creature, and where do his ancestors come from? The Syrian hamster is one of the most popular of a few types of hamsters that are notably good as pets. After all, who can resist a furry creature with big eyes and tiny paws and a name like teddy bear? The other types of popular hamsters are the Campbell's dwarf hamsters, and Russian dwarf hamsters. The most notable difference between the Syrian and the dwarf hamster is the size, though some of their social habits differ, also.

Syrian hamsters belong to the *Mesocricetus auratus* species, Adar's family history as a pet in North America is a relatively short one. There are several versions of the discovery of the Syrian hamster by outsiders, but the most recorded version is that the Syrian hamster was classified and named in 1839 by a young British zoologist named George Robert Waterhouse. Waterhouse, a curator for the London Zoological society, treated the hamster as though it was a new species of hamster and named the hamster *Cricetus auratus*— golden hamster. It was not until 1902 that Nehring studied the Syrian hamster and re-classified it as *Mesocricetus auratus,* but the classification given by Waterhouse stuck and was used for many years even after the re-classification.

While the classifications may be of little importance to the pet owner, it separates the types of hamsters according to their distinct characteristics, which can be important for preservation of a particular species and for breeding purposes. In 1940, Ellerman noted the differences between *Mesocricetus* and *Cricetus.* He stated that the distinct differences were the tail length, overall size, and litter size. From that time, scientists and breeders have correctly referred to the Syrian hamster as *Mesocricetus auratus.*

Even though Waterhouse named the hamster, he was not the first to discover and write something about the Syrian hamster. In 1797, *The Natural History of Aleppo* contained a description of the hamster, but did not list a new classification and name. Waterhouse classified and named the hamster, as well as showed its skull and skin to the Zoological Society of London. According to some reports, the hamster skin and skull still reside at the British Museum of Natural History.

Around 1880, James Henry Skeen took care of a colony of Syrian hamsters in Edinburgh, Scotland, but that colony died out about 30 years later.

So how did the little creature become so popular and widespread? In 1930, Israel Aharoni, a Hebrew zoologist, went on

13

an expedition to the Aleppo region. At the request of Saul Alder, a colleague and parasitologist who used hamsters for research, he looked for and found, with the help of others, a nest with a female and eleven pups. The newborn pups' eyes were not yet open, giving the opportunity for the hamsters to be observed from a very young age. Once in captivity, the mother hamster killed one of the babies, and the mother died. Another baby escaped, but Aharoni and his wife were able to care for the nine remaining babies, until they delivered the hamsters to Hein Ben-Menachen, the head of the Hebrew University Animal Facilities on Mt. Scopas.

Ben-Menachen made the mistake of putting the clever hamsters in a cage with a wooden floor, and five of them found their way out of the cage and disappeared. Of the remaining hamsters, two mated, and as it is with hamsters, within a year, there were over 150 hamsters!

Some of the hamsters that were bred in the laboratory were sent to Alder. Alder sent hamsters on to other labs in other countries, and in 1931, the Syrian hamster made it to England. The story is that Alder sneaked the hamsters into England in his coat pockets. There, a British protozoologist, Leonard George Goodwin, bred and used the hamsters as test hamsters for research. The furry little hamsters made their way into the hearts and homes of the people, and the rest is, as they say, *history*.

© Roman Sigaev @Fotolia

2: A Close-Up View of the Syrian Hamster

Syrian hamsters come in many colors and patterns. Some confusion surrounds the Syrian hamster name for this reason. Pet shop owners often choose names that describe the color or pattern of the hamster, rather than the correct name. This is understandable, as it makes it simple for shoppers. You can find Syrian hamsters called names such as *black bear*, *teddy bear*, or *panda bear*. It's important to remember that these are just names given to Syrian hamsters based on their looks, and they are not a different species. Therefore, the care and health of the Syrian hamster applies.

For better understanding, let's sort out some of the many coats, colors, and patterns of the Syrian hamster.

Syrian Hamster Coats

Longhaired or Shorthaired

There are both longhaired and shorthaired Syrian hamsters. Due to their wispy hair, longhaired hamsters look puffier than their shorthaired counterparts look.

The longhaired version comes from a recessive gene, which means that you have to mate two longhaired hamsters to get a longhaired hamster. The male longhaired has a particularly long coat, as the longer hair is caused by the higher level of testosterone. The female longhair coat is only minimally longer than a shorthaired hamster coat. The male longhaired hamster requires careful cleaning, which is discussed in a later chapter of this guide.

Shorthaired hamsters look velvety, and perhaps a bit more refined than the longhaired ones, if human traits were applied to the little creatures. The shorthaired coat appears to have more shine, and it does not become matted as easily as the longhaired coat.

Satin Coat

Syrian hamsters have either a satin coat or non-satin coat. As the name implies, the satin coat is glossy. The satin coat gene is dominant, so it does not require the breeding of two satin-coat hamsters to produce a satin-coat hamster. In fact, breeders say it is not a good idea to breed to satin-coat Syrians together, as the result is often a pup with poor-looking thin fur.

Rex Coat

You may have seen hamsters with curly or wavy coats and slightly curled whiskers. These hamsters sport a rex coat. If you want a rex-coat hamster, you must breed two rex-coat hamsters to get a rex-coat pup, as the rex gene is recessive.

Syrian Coat Patterns

Banded

When you visit a pet store, you will probably mostly see the banded pattern Syrian hamster. The banded pattern hamster looks almost like they are wearing a polo shirt with wide, though undefined stripes. For show purposes, the perfect band coat would have a defined band one-third of the width of the hamster body, right in the middle of the body. However, this perfect showmanship banding is usually not the case. The banding of the coat is not predictable in breeding.

Dominant Spotted

As if a hamster needed anything to make it cuter and more playful, some boast a coat of spots! Spots are particularly common for hamsters that are golden, black, or cinnamon colored. For showmanship, the dominant spotted hamster should look like a white hamster with evenly dispersed spots over the coat. But in most cases, hamster coats have anywhere from a few random spots to so many that the main color of the coat doesn't show much at all.

Roan

In the human hair world, the roan hamster coat would be described as *ombre*. Ombre is a hair color style where the hair is darker at the roots and gets lighter with the length of the hair. With the roan hamster coat, the fur is usually darker at the head and lightens over the length of the hamster body. With some roan coats, the color shade is significant, and with others, it is subtle.

Hamsters with roan coats can sometimes be identified by the reddish glow of the eyes when the eyes are exposed to light. The reddish glow of the eye can also be a sign that the hamster carries the Wh gene, known as the white belly gene. However, some hamsters that do not have the Wh gene, still have a red tint to their eyes.

Breeders recommend that two roans are never mated, as they produce pups with deformities such as being born without eyes and teeth.

Tortoise Shell

Tortoiseshell hamsters have two colors of fur, a main color and a coordinating yellow color. The color splotches are distributed in a pattern over the body, and the identifier is the splotches of yellow color. Only female hamsters are tortoise shell.

Coat Colors

Syrian hamsters wear many coats of many colors! There are dozens of colors and color combinations. Hamsters have their own built-in fashion sense with specific eye, ear, and coat color coordination. Hamster hair is a darker color at the base and immediately lighter so that the base color barely shows unless you look at the roots of the fur. The base darker color is known as *ticking.*

In the color descriptions, when the cheek crescent and cheek flash are mentioned, it is referring to distinct cheek areas that are marked by color. In simple terms, the cheek flash is the area of the hamster that would be the collar area, and extending into the cheek area on a person. The flash area runs from a little below the ear and up and around neck. The cheek crescent is the area that marks around the nose and below the chin that extends up into the puffy cheek area of the hamster's face.

There are far too many colors and color combinations to list every one in detail in this book. Below is a list of the common colors for Syrian hamsters, with more description for the classic golden. The colors are listed in no particular order.

Golden: A golden hamster's coat is a classic golden blonde color, and the coordinating ear color is gray. The golden has black eyes and has some black on the cheek flash and some white on the cheek crescent. At the base of each individual hair, the color is slate gray.

Agouti Varieties
Honey
Beige
Blonde

Yellow
Cinnamon
Gray—dark, light, and silver
Lilac
Smoke Pearl
Rust

Self Varieties
Black
Chocolate
Dove
Mink
Sable
Copper
Cream
White
White albino

Hamster Size and Characteristics

Hamsters are what they are---cute and furry, with a small body that works perfectly for them when they are in good health.

In general, Syrian hamsters have cylindrical bodies and are about six to eight inches long, and they weigh in at about three to five ounces. Of course, their weight and size can vary. Dwarf hamsters are smaller hamsters than the Syrian golden hamster.

The most prominent physical feature of a hamster is probably their classic rodent-type teeth. The hamster's teeth, one pair of upper incisors and a pair of lower incisors, are their means of survival. The teeth continue to grow as the hamster ages. Though it may sound a bit silly, dental care is critical for hamsters. If their teeth are not aligned properly and kept whittled down by their gnawing on wood, they can literally starve to death. Chew sticks are high on the hamster's shopping list!

It is easy to tell the male hamster from the female, as the male develops testicles on each side of the anus around the fourth or fifth week of its life, and the testicles are visible to the observer. Also, if you examine the hamster, you can tell that in the male hamster the distance between the anus and the sexual opening is considerably more than the same area on the female hamster. Though a more subtle sign, a side-view of the hindquarters can help you determine the sex of the hamster. Males have a more elongated hindquarter than females.

It is a common misnomer that hamsters are nocturnal. They are not, even though they may choose to be awake and play at night sometimes. Hamsters are actually crepuscular. Crepusculum is a Latin word that means "twilight." A hamster's most active times are dawn and dusk. It makes sense that hamsters would forage about during the early morning hours, having the advantage of daylight to scout for food, but not having the disadvantage of nocturnal predators.

The Syrian Hamster's Body

Ears

A hamster's ears are tiny and give it an overall cuteness, but they also serve a purpose. In the wild, hamsters needed a strong sense of hearing to detect animals that would prefer them for lunch, long before said predators were close enough to give chase to the hamster. It is believed that the hamster's sense of hearing is so developed that they can hear sounds in the ultrasonic frequencies, and for this reason they can communicate with one another without other animals hearing them.

Eyes

On the other hand, hamsters do not have a keen sense of sight. By human standards, they seem to be somewhat nearsighted, meaning they cannot focus on objects that are very close to their face. However, they do have good peripheral vision and can see for some distance. Though it is not known for certain, it is believed that hamsters are color blind, so the bright primary colors of the hamster wheels and toys are probably more for the enjoyment of the hamster owner than the hamster.

Nose

21

If you have ever held a hamster after you have had food in your hands, you know by the way they nibble on your fingers as though they can extract the food they smell from them, that hamsters have a good sense of smell. It is always a good idea to wash your hands before handling your hamster.

Hamsters seem to recognize their owners by the person's scent, also. If you want your hamster to recognize you, hold them often so they develop familiarity with your scent.

Teeth

Their teeth are what get hamsters officially classified as rodents. Believe it or not, the tiny hamster mouth holds four incisors (front teeth) and eight molars. The hamster's teeth continue to grow throughout their life, and they will become too long if the hamster does not consistently gnaw on hard objects to help file down the teeth. The hamster is born with white teeth, but the teeth will soon become yellowed. This is a natural occurrence and not due to poor dental health or a lack of hygiene.

Whiskers

Besides their rodent-like teeth, hamsters also have whiskers on their face and on the side of their body that give them the classic rodent look. The whiskers serve a purpose, allowing the hamster to navigate its way around objects when it is scampering or when the objects are close up and they might not see them clearly. You may not even notice the whiskers on the side of the body, as they blend it with the fur.

Cheek Pouches

In the way of cheek pouches, hamsters have built-in storage areas for their food. When they forage for food, they put the food in their cheek pouches so it can be easily transported and reserved until needed. The pouches are amazingly perfect for storing food and keeping it dry, as saliva and digestive liquids from the mouth do not get into the cheek pouches. The skin of the hamster's cheeks is lined with a rough material that is similar to slightly crinkled leather. The design and texture of the cheek pouches keeps the store food from moving into the hamster's mouth.

If you think those pouches look pretty puffy, it may be because the hamster can pack food that is almost half of their body weight in their cheek pouches!

Hip Glands

On each side of their body, in the hip area, hamsters have glands. The glands are covered by fur, and not noticeable if you are not looking for them. The glands secrete an oily substance that is used to mark their territory, much in the same way that Fido raises his leg and marks his territory. In the wild, the Syrian hamster marks their burrow by rubbing against the wall of the burrow and causing the gland to secrete the marking oil.

© Ilike @Fotolia

Hamsters Make Great Pets

Children usually adore hamsters, and often choose them for their first pet. Mom and Dad think this is a good thing since hamsters require less space and care than a puppy or kitten. They eat a lot less food, and their food is not expensive. Some prominent hamster publications have touted hamsters as the perfect pet and a survey conducted by the American Pet Products Manufacturers Association showed that hamsters consistently rank high as the most popular small pet.

Hamsters are perfect for apartment dwellers or those who spend the day away from home. They are inexpensive, easy to acquire, and compact. They do not have to be walked on a leash or let in and out of the house to do their thing. In fact, hamsters prefer to stay away from noise and traffic, but probably enjoy a little sunshine out in the quiet yard.

Hamsters do not bark at neighbors, or jump up on guests at the door. Nor do they leave fur on the furniture or dig in flowerbeds. Well, maybe they would burrow in flowerbeds if given the chance, but at least it would be a very small hole.

When given proper care and attention, hamsters are odor-free and clean; thus wonderful little pets for children to hold and cuddle. Children usually make good hamster owners because they enjoy spending time with their hamster. With their silly antics and shenanigans, hamsters can entertain children and adults.

Hamsters may not be classified as man's best friend, but the furry creatures make excellent pets for any person who is willing to take the responsibility and time, which is not much, to keep them happily fed, housed, and protected. Read on to find out how you can do just that!

The one thing that makes hamster a difficult pet for children and adults is that they have such a short lifespan. The average lifespan for a hamster is only about two to two and one-half years. This is assuming the hamster is healthy and well taken care of. Unlike a dog that can be with a family for over a decade, hamsters should be considered a temporary pet.

Before you purchase a hamster for a child, it is important to have a talk with them about the short life span of a hamster. In general, children accept this fact, and to some children two years may seem like a long time, but some may prefer to avoid becoming emotionally attached to a pet that will be only be with them for a short period.

When you have the talk about the short lifespan, also emphasize that good care is critical for a hamster's well being, but that even with the best of care hamsters sometimes become sick for unknown reasons and can die before they reach their lifespan. If something does cause the hamster to die prematurely, you do not want the child to think it is their fault if they have been properly caring for the hamster.

In the event that the hamster gets sick with cancer or another chronic or terminal disease, or becomes severely injured, the humane thing to do is have it euthanized so that it does not suffer. If this happens, you need to be honest about it with your child. Explain to the child why the euthanization is necessary and that it is the best thing for the hamster. The child will probably become emotional and need some time to process their emotions. It may be difficult for them to come to terms with losing their pet. During the process, they may even accuse you of "killing" their hamster. Don't take it personally. Continue to talk to them about how it is best not to let the hamster suffer, and tell them how sorry you are for the loss they feel.

A talk about the hamster life span may bring up questions. Your child may want to know what happens to the hamster when it dies. They may ask if hamsters go to heaven. If the child has attended a funeral or seen a gravesite before, they may ask if hamsters are put in a grave. It's best to think about the answers ahead of time so you can give them answers that line up with your belief system.

If you have your hamster euthanized, the veterinarian will take care of the disposal of the pet, unless you request to take the pet home so you can bury it. Disposal is handled differently at different vet offices, so discuss this matter with your specific vet.

In most cases, when a hamster dies, it is buried in the family yard. Depending on your belief system, you may want to arrange a simple ceremony that marks the passing of the hamster and allows the children to "say goodbye."

Before You Purchase a Hamster for a Child

- Talk about the responsibility of keeping it safe and well taken care of

- Talk about the short life span

Below is a checklist for your review before you purchase a hamster.

Considerations before Shopping for a Hamster

o   **Do I have a good spot for the hamster habitat?** Keep in mind that your hamster probably won't be on the same sleeping schedule as you are, unless you have an usual sleeping schedule. Your hamster may choose to play during the wee hours of the morning or just about the time you go to bed at night, when you are trying to sleep. This may mean that you do not want the hamster in your bedroom.

o   **Are there toddlers in the house?** Toddlers have a mind of their own, but their thinking is not yet developed enough to think things through, such as opening the hamster cage door and letting it escape. Can your hamster cage be put in a place where the toddler can't stick their fingers in the cage and get bitten? There is no reason to not purchase a hamster if there is a toddler in the household, but it is a consideration.

o   **Is anyone in the household allergic to animal fur?** For the most part, hamsters do not seem to be a big allergen problem. However, if you or someone in your household is allergic to other animal fur, it is worth noting that they may also be allergic to hamster fur.

o   **Do you have anyone to take care of your hamster when you go on vacation or need to be away from home for a few days?** Hamsters and their homes are portable, so you may be able to take your hamster on some vacations with you. For instance, if you are staying in a cottage at the sea for the summer, your hamster could probably tag along with no problems as long as you kept it comfortable, protected, fed, and watered on the trip. But there will likely be times when you vacation or leave home and it is not appropriate or safe to take your hamster with you. Do you have a few trustworthy people in mind that you could leave your hamster with?

○ **Does your schedule allow the time to take care of your hamster?** Hamsters do not require a lot of time, but they certainly cannot be put on a shelf and forgotten when you get busy. Hamsters prefer human company to other hamster company, but they need to be socialized and that requires some time for holding and playing with the hamster. Your hamster also needs sanitary living conditions at all times, which means you must be available to clean their cage and take care of any sanitation issues as needed.

© Leonid Nyshko @ Fotolia

3: The Longhaired Syrian Hamster

The longhaired Syrian Hamster, also known as the teddy bear hamster, is the sweetheart of hamsters. With its bright round eyes, chubby cheeks, tiny button nose, and fluffy, long hair, it captures the hamster lovers heart even beyond all other hamsters.

The long hair that makes the longhaired Syrian hamster so adorable also makes it just a bit unique. The selection of and care for the Syrian hamster is mostly universal, but there are just a few extra considerations with the longhaired hamster.

The teddy bear hamster requires special attention for his coat. Because of the length of the fur, bedding and whatever the hamster encounters sticks to the fur. If special care is not given, the coat will give the hamster a disheveled and unclean look, similar to that of a child who has been playing outside all day, out of the reach of their mother's washcloth and hairbrush.

Shorthaired hamsters do very well with grooming themselves, but the longhaired teddy bear hamster needs some assistance with their coat to obtain their best look and remain clean. For this purpose, you need to schedule a weekly (or more often if preferred) grooming session for brushing the hamster and making sure the body is clean, especially around the rear end. Pet stores carry a special soft-bristled brush for brushing the hamster, although any small soft-bristled brush works fine. Some find that a new toothbrush with soft bristles works perfectly because of its small brush size and long handle for easy holding.

Before brushing the hamster, remove it from its cage and gently pick out all of the bedding and debris that has accumulated in the fur. When you brush the hamster, hold it with care and gently stroke it with the brush, without squeezing the hamster or putting any pressure on the brush. The hamster probably will not like their grooming sessions, particularly at first, but after they find that you are not going to hurt them, they should settle into the weekly routine. They may even start to look forward to their grooming session with you.

Hamsters are not water animals. They may get into their water dish and play a bit, but they are highly susceptible to illness if they get wet and cold. You should never bathe any hamster in the traditional sense of immersing the hamster in water or soaking it with water. Bathing also removes the natural protective oils from the hamster's skin.

The stress alone of bathing could make a hamster sick, not to mention that the slightest draft could cause a wet hamster to catch a cold. If conditions were right, a wet, cold hamster would also be vulnerable to diseases such as wet tail.

> **Never bathe your longhair Syrian hamster by immersing it in water!**

Hamsters are good groomers without much help from their owners. If your longhaired hamster needs a bath, you can give it a sand bath. In the wild, Syrian hamsters live in the dessert and make tunnels in the sand. The sand rubs against their fur and cleans it; much like a scrubbing pad that uses abrasion to clean a dirty surface.

If your mischievous hamster gets into something sticky or dirty and has a few spots on their coat that need to be cleaned, you can use a cotton swab dipped in warm water to clean a spot or two off the hamster every now and then. Again, don't get the coat wet! And don't use a blow dryer to dry the fur unless you want to scare the poor hamster to death!

For the sand bath, fill a small container with taller sides (to prevent your hamster from escaping) with a couple of inches of very fine sand. Do not use just any sand that you find outside or at the beach. Go to the pet store and purchase fine sand that is specifically for bathing small animals that should not take water baths. Put your hamster in the sand and let it frolic and roll around. If there are special areas on the hamster that need more effort, gently rub those areas with sand. Never put any force behind the rubbing. To do so would make your hamster feel as though you are using sand paper on it, and you could damage the skin.

Longhaired hamsters, particularly males, can have problems with getting urine on their fur when they urinate or droppings when they poop. Check for this problem, and if you notice it, wet a cotton swab and gently clean the affected area. Do not soak the swab so that it gets a large area wet. Just gently dab the swab on the precise affected area.

While the longhaired hamster coat is adorable, if it becomes too unwieldy or if something becomes stuck in it that you cannot remove without causing the hamster discomfort, you may need to trim the fur. If you trim the fur, use sharp, small scissors. Short hair cutting scissors work perfectly. Of course, you must be extremely careful when trimming. Make sure your hamster is calm and still. Do not attempt to trim it when it wants to be active or when you are in a hurry. If you make a regular habit of handling and grooming the hamster, it should not be a big ordeal to give it a little trim now and again.

30

With all of that hair, it can be difficult to notice any abrasions or other skin problems. This means you need to be extra careful to check for skin irritation, abrasions, and bald spots each time you groom your longhaired Syrian hamster. As with all hamsters, also check its paws and claws, and make sure the claws are not turning under. Keep the claws trimmed as needed. You can trim them with a special pet nail clipper or use a small clipper designed for cutting human baby fingernails.

As has been stated in this guide, the best way to assure that your hamster stays clean is to keep its environment clean. Never fail to change the bedding and clean the cage thoroughly each week. Never allow your longhaired hamster, or any other hamster, to live in soiled or wet bedding.

© Aramanda @ Fotolia

4: Choose Your Syrian Hamster

It's just a hamster, right? So what's the big deal about hamster shopping? Don't you just go to the pet store, pick out one, and take it home? First, it's going to be *your* hamster or a hamster for someone you care about. It can be very disappointing if the hamster you choose has a shorter than normal lifespan. At best, the lifespan of a healthy hamster is only about two years. A weak or sick hamster can die suddenly, especially without the proper care. So to avoid the disappointment of getting a sick or old hamster, there are some things you should know. You will find out about those things in this chapter.

Where to Shop for a Hamster

After you have decided what kind of hamster you want, you have a few options as to where you may get the hamster. Since hamsters reproduce often and have a short gestation period, there are usually plenty of them to go around. You may have friends, classmates, co-workers, or other acquaintances that have baby hamsters to sell or give away. Another option is the local animal shelter where lost hamsters that have been captured or hamsters that have been taken to the shelter when their owner could no longer take care of them are up for adoption. If you have a county or state fair in your area, you may be able to find hamster breeders there, as hamster breeders often show their prize hamsters in fair competitions.

The most common option is to purchase the hamster from a local breeder or a local pet store. If you do not have a local pet store or breeder and do not have other mentioned options, ask local veterinarians if they know of a good source for hamsters.

The important thing is that you get your hamster from a reputable source. Unfortunately, some people run hamster mills, meaning they carelessly breed a large number of hamsters for the sheer purpose of making money, and they do not provide premium care for the hamsters. Crowded conditions, poor nutrition, improper breeding practices, and lack of attention to details in the care and feeding of the hamster can result in sickly, weak hamsters.

Carefully check out the environment for answers to these questions:

✓ Are the hamsters separated in their own cage or are several housed in the same small cage?

✓ Does the bedding in the cage look clean and is it free of urine odor?

✓ Does the cage have exercise toys in it?

✓ Do the owner and/or employees seem to care about the hamsters?

✓ Do the owner and/or employees seem to be knowledgeable about hamsters, and able to answer your questions?

✓ Are the owner and/or employees willing to answer questions about the hamsters' health, recent disease in their shop, and the age of the hamster?

✓ Does the store look clean in general?

Tips for Buying a Healthy, Happy Hamster

When you go to buy a hamster, do not be shy about asking questions and picking up the hamster and examining it very closely. A knowledgeable hamster breeder will be happy to answer your questions, and may even have a few questions for you to be assured that you will be a good owner for their hamsters.

Before you go, make sure you know what you want to look for when you examine the hamsters. In fact, take this guide with you and go through the checklist below to make sure you do not forget anything.

If you come across a shop owner that does not want you to pick up a hamster, politely explain that you will gladly wash your hands or wear disposable gloves, but you would like to examine the hamster before considering a purchase. You may even suggest that they pick up the hamster and hold it close enough to you for you to examine. If they refuse a close-up examination, they may have a reason that they do not want you to examine the hamster up close, and it's best to mark that shop or breeder off your list.

Check the Hamster's Health

✓ **Check for wet tail.** Wet tail is a serious, contagious bacterial infection that is common in hamsters. When not properly treated, wet tail often results in the death of hamsters. (There is more information on wet tail in the health chapter of this book.) To check a hamster for wet tail, look at the fur underneath the tail and see if it is dry and the fur is the same color there as the rest of the hamster fur in that area. If the fur is wet or stained, it is a sign that the hamster has or has had wet tail or diarrhea. If you see loose, watery droppings in the cage, it is also a sign of wet tail.

If you see signs of wet tail, it's probably best not to get your hamster from that store or breeder. The contagious nature of the infection makes wet tail hard to control once it gets started and is passed around.

✓ **Check for lethargy.** In general, hamsters are spunky little creatures. Even when they are not moving, there is activeness about them. If you observe that the hamsters in a shop are lethargic, you will want to skip those hamsters. Most likely they are not well taken care of or are sick if they are lethargic.

✓ **Check the hamster's teeth.** As mentioned earlier, a hamster depends on the proper teeth alignment and the correct length in order to eat and survive. To check a hamster's teeth, gently lift the hamster and turn it on its back. With the other hand, gently grasp the hamster's fur on the back of its neck ruff. When you gently tug on the fur, the hamster will open its mouth and you can get a look at its teeth. (Do not worry, this does not hurt the hamster if done gently.)

The hamster's teeth, which continue to grow throughout the lifetime of the hamster, should not be curled or too long. If they are extraordinarily long, it is a sign that the hamster may not have been given the appropriate chew food or wood sticks to gnaw to help whittle down the teeth. Or it could be a sign that the hamster has not received a necessary filing or clipping of the teeth. The bottom front teeth should be shorter than the top front teeth. Do not expect the hamster's teeth to be pearly whites. When they are very young babies, they still have the white

teeth that they are born with, but the teeth yellow quickly.
They will appear yellowed or slightly browned.
Your hamster should have four incisors (front teeth) and
eight molars. If any of the teeth are brittle or broken, it
could signify health problems.

✓ **Check for pregnancy.** If a hamster is pregnant, you will
see a bulge in the abdominal region below the rib cage. You
may also be able to see protruded nipples. Also, ask the
shop owner or employee if the hamster has had the
opportunity to mate at any time since it reached five weeks
old.

✓ **Check for scrapes, bites, and missing tail and ear parts.**
You do not want to buy a hamster that has been involved in
fights with other hamsters. Even if that hamster isn't the
aggressor, fighting and abuse can stress the hamster and
change its temperament. Stress also seems to cause the
hamster to be skittish and more aggressive.

✓ **Take a look at the nose.** The hamster's nose should be
barely moist but not wet, and not dripping with any
discharge. Discharge from the nose can mean the hamster
has a cold or infection or is allergic to something in the
cage.

✓ **Check the eyes.** When you look closely at the hamster's
eyes, what you really want to see is…nothing. The eyes
should be clear and bright. You don't want to see a haze
over the eyes or a sty around the eyelid, or any type of
discharge or weepiness.

✓ **Check for parasites.** When proper care is given, hamsters
are not prone to external parasites such as mites. To check
for fleas part the fur and look at the skin. The skin should
be smooth and not bumpy, irritated, or flaky.

✓ **Be aware of Syrian hamster scent glands.** They Syrian hamster has scent glands on the side of each hip. The glands are marked by dark moles.

✓ **Check the overall body shape.** The hamster body shape should be cylindrical and completely filled out. It should have a solid look, rather than a fragile look. It should look a bit like an evenly-stuffed pillow, without hollow areas or big bulges in the main part of the body.

✓ **Check for lumps.** If you find lumps on the hamster's body, it could mean the hamster has something as serious as cancerous growth or as minor as a mild infection or ulcer, which can be treated with antibiotics. It is best to pass on any hamster that has lumps on its body. There is no good reason for a healthy hamster to have lumps on the body.

✓ **Check the gender!** Before you go shopping for a hamster, decide if you want a male or female hamster. Obviously, if you want to breed hamsters, you will need to get one of each.

How much does a Hamster Cost?

Syrian hamsters are not expensive, but the price for a hamster can vary, depending on where it is purchased and your geographical location. Some shop keepers may also charge a little more for the most popular sellers or base their price on how many hamsters they have in stock. In general, hamsters usually cost around $20USD or £12 UK. Breeders usually charge more for quality "show" hamsters.

When you count the financial cost of your hamster, remember that the purchase price is not your only cost. Your hamster will need a safe place to call home, exercise equipment, food, water bottle, and other miscellaneous items. Don't forget to set aside funds for emergency vet care, as well. Even with those considerations, the hamster is not a high-maintenance or expensive pet.

Have a Safe Trip Home

When you purchase your hamster, make sure it is secured in a breathable container for the trip to its new home. If the weather is very hot or cold, anything other than comfortably mild, do not leave your hamster in its travel container in the car while you go other places. Your new friend will probably already be a bit nervous, so the sooner you get them to their new environment, the better. Hamsters have a keen sense of hearing and do not like loud noises. Keep this in mind as you travel home with your hamster.

And speaking of their new home, read on so you know how to provide the perfect habitat for your hamster.

© Andy Lidstone @Fotolia

5: Make Your Hamster Feel at Home

There is nothing so wonderful as the comfort of home. A place where you have everything you need and can relax and have a happy life. Adar and Annie Hamster know this too! In this chapter, they are your guides for choosing a quality hamster abode for your new pet.

In choosing a habitat for the Syrian hamster, it can be helpful to think about their natural life in the wild. What comforts do they seek? What do they need for protection? Adar's Syrian hamster family lives in the sandy desert areas where there is not much food available. Like most rodent-like animals, a good deal of their time is spent scavenging for food that can be taken back to a room in their burrow. Female Syrian hamsters fill their cheek pouches with food that can be stored for when she gives birth to a litter of pups. In the wild, Syrian hamsters eat grains, grass, seeds, wild fruit if it can be found, roots, stems, and small insects and worms.

It is not practical to think that the habitat of the wild Syrian hamster will be duplicated exactly for the domesticated hamster that is a house pet, but you can get a better idea of what might seem natural to your hamster. You can create a living space where your hamster can forage for food, go through tunnels that might be similar to tunnels in the wild, and exercise frequently. You can provide interesting terrain for your hamster to explore by taking it out of the cage daily and letting in explore different areas. Remember, to such a small animal, even the corner of a room is a large space, so don't lit it have too much freedom to run too far.

It's best to shop for your hamster cage, food, and necessities before you bring your hamster home. Having the cage ready for your hamster can lower the risk of your it escaping or getting injured until you get the cage and get it ready.

Here are some tips for preparing just the right home for your hamster.

The Cage

The cage, where your hamster will spend the majority of their time, is the biggest and most important investment for your hamster. If you want to have more than one hamster, you should count on having a separate cage and set-up for each hamster.

There are a couple of ways to obtain a hamster cage. You can purchase one from a pet store or animal supply store, or if you are handy with a few basic tools and carpentry skills, you can also make a cage. If you decide to make your cage, you have the option of designing it with fun nooks and crannies for your hamster to enjoy games of hide and seek. However, the materials for a homemade cage are of concern. Keep this in mind for cage safety, practicality, and longevity.

Homemade Cages

Homemade cages can be custom designed with nooks and crannies where your hamster can hide and play. However, an important feature of the cage design, whether homemade or bought, is the ease in cleaning the cage. Ease of cleaning, and whether it will retain odors should be considered when selecting material for the cage. Particleboard should not be used for building a hamster home, as it contains toxic glue that can lead to serious illness or death of the hamster.

Often, homemade cages are made from wood for the frame, with fine mesh wire sides, and a mesh wire top, and a removable metal or hard plastic tray that sits on the bottom of the cage. Wood is not the ideal material for a hamster home, but can work if only used for the frame of the cage. Hamsters will gnaw on wood and wood can retain odors.

The cage must be escape-proof, for the hamster is able to escape through the smallest of openings the very minute that you turn your back! And never under estimate the strength of a tiny hamster when it comes to lifting a top off a cage. One of the best safeguards for keeping hamsters in their cage is to set up a home

©CallallooAlexis @ Fotolia

where the hamster has everything they need, and where they are comfortable. This does not mean they won't occasionally get mischievous and break out, but it does mean that, for the most part, they will stay in their cage unless taken out.

Of course, the cage must be safe; free from sharp or jagged edges, and free from any place where the hamster could get stuck. If the cage is made from wood, you must check constantly for splintering. Due to the fact that wood absorbs moisture, you must be diligent in checking unsealed wood cages for moisture where mold can grow.

The cage must protect your hamster from cats or other animals that would snatch it from its habitat. The cage should also be weather appropriate for the space that it will be in and for the climate in which you live. For instance, if you live in a hot climate, such as Arizona, and have the cage in a sunny room, a glass aquarium is probably not the best home for your hamster. Instead, you would choose a well-ventilated cage with good air circulation.

Given their size, and that they will exercise in their exercise wheel or ball, a hamster does not need a huge cage. They do need enough space to enjoy their habit of separating their areas for eating, sleeping, and going to the bathroom. Hamsters are tidy little creatures, so once you set up their home, they seem to understand the system and do a good job of keeping it organized. Hamster breeders and owners seem to agree that hamsters need a home that is about 16x12x10 inches or 40x30x25 cm.

Buying a Previously Used Cage

Hamster cages are standard fare at summer garage sales and at thrift stores. Hamsters have a short life span, and once the hamster is gone, the owners donate the cage for someone else to use. While there is nothing wrong with saving money and buying a used cage, you should remember that one reason the cage may be available is that the housed hamster may have died of disease. For this reason, it is very important to thoroughly wash and disinfect the cage before putting in any of the hamster's food or water dishes, bedding, supplies, or toys. Another consideration is that some plastics are more apt to retain odor and germs more readily than glass or metal. So put your sniffer to work and make sure the cage does not have residual odors.

Because of common hamster bacterial diseases such as wet tail, it is recommended that a strong disinfectant be used to clean used cages. Make sure the cage is rinsed thoroughly and there is no residue of disinfectant. Of course, if you have a cage where you have previously housed a sick hamster, the same procedure should be followed.

Glass Aquarium Style Cages

With a tightly fitting lid that easily slides off and on, a glass aquarium-style cage may be the most escape-free home for your hamster. With this type of cage, there are no bars for hamsters to squeeze between, and no door that can be accidentally left unlatched. Do not forget that there are plenty of hamster stories about hamsters learning to unlatch the door of their cage!

A ten-gallon or larger aquarium with a tight-fitting, metal-framed lid with a meshed screen top is secure and provides ample ventilation for your hamster. Again, it is advisable not to put the glass aquarium, or any cage for that matter, where the sun will beat directly down on it. The glass will heat up considerably and make your hamster feel as though they are living in a green house or sauna. Condensation will create moisture inside the cage and the risk of mold and bad bacteria growth is increased. A moist habitat can also increase the risk of the hamster developing respiratory ailments.

A glass cage is easy to keep clean, and the solid walls help keep the bedding inside the cage instead of strewn around the outside of the cage. The solid walls also create a barrier against the long arm of the cat or other creatures on the prowl for a hamster dinner. On the other hand, the same walls create a less airy habitat for your hamster.

While aquariums are safe and sturdy homes for hamsters, there are a few drawbacks. There is an outside chance that the aquarium can be broken if dropped or hit hard with another object. Because they are heavy, they can be hard for children to lift and clean. With this in mind, it's best if an adult transports the cage to a utility sink or outside for thorough cleaning. The rigid, tall sides of the cage may also make it difficult for younger children to reach inside the cage to retrieve their hamster.

Old aquariums may be sealed with putty type material rather than silicon that is now used for sealant. Some putty contains lead, which is not safe for your hamster to ingest. Keep in mind that if it is there, there is a good chance that your hamster will find it and nibble on it. There is no hiding anything from those curious little creatures. Therefore, unless you are certain that your old aquarium is sealed with silicon and not putty, it's best not to use it for your hamster's home.

Wire Cages

Traditional wire cages are simple by design and make a great home for your hamster. They usually have a slide-out bottom tray that makes cleaning the cage easy, and the barred walls allow you to touch and interact with your hamster while he is caged. Wire cages provide excellent ventilation to help keep bedding dry and mold-free. The bars on a wire cage should run horizontally, rather than vertically, and be between 3/8 and ½ inches or 1-1.3 cm apart.

The open style of the wire cage allows your hamster to create a mess with their bedding and food on the outside of the cage. For that reason, you may prefer to set the cage on an easy-clean mat or tray, particularly if you want to protect the furniture or flooring beneath the cage.

If your hamster seems to think it is happier in the outside world and tries to escape at every given opportunity, you may want to secure the door with an added wire twist tie that the hamster cannot chew through.

Plastic Habitats

All types of plastic hamster cages can be found at pet supply stores. The cage packaging usually consists of pictures of adorable hamsters that play happily in their brightly colored modern home that is designed to somewhat mimic their natural habitat. Naturally, children are drawn to these pictures and may want to choose their hamster cage based on the pictures.

The plastic cages and their matching accessories such as tubes, are molded plastic. Some of them are one-piece designs, while some of them come in modular pieces that can be taken apart for easy cleaning or for adding other pieces. Most plastic cages are sturdy, but they can still be cracked or chipped if accidentally dropped on a hard surface, and they are easily scratched, meaning that within a short time the cage looks old. The elaborate plastic cages with various components come with a hefty price tag compared to other, simpler, traditional types of cages.

Though it is not common, in some instances hamsters have been known to chew through the plastic. Not only does this allow the hamster to escape, but the hamster can develop severe digestive problems from chewing the plastic.

The plastic modules can be difficult to take apart for cleaning, especially for children. This is a setback because one of the reasons parents want their children to have a small, manageable pet is to teach them the responsibility of taking care of a pet on their own. If the adult has to take responsibility for cleaning the cage, this benefit is lost. The plastic cages can also retain unpleasant urine odors that are difficult to remove once they are there.

Multi-tiered Habitats

There is mixed reviewed about two or three-story hamster homes. Some say that it provides more interesting play and livelihood for the hamster, while others say that hamsters are not great climbers and the height poses the risk of the hamster falling and sustaining injuries. One solution to this problem might be to provide secure miniature ladders to make it easier for the hamster to access the top levels of the house.

Necessary Supplies for the Hamster Home

Bedding

Hamsters are burrowing animals, and in captivity, it is necessary for them to have burrowing material in their cage. That is where cage bedding comes in. The idea behind bedding is to provide burrowing material and to keep the cage dry and comfortable for the hamster. There are various kinds of commercial bedding. Hamster bedding can be made from cedar, pine, or aspen wood, as well as vegetable material and paper. It's best to avoid bedding with a strong scent, even though manufacturers of such bedding advertise it as an odor retardant bedding. This includes natural cedar bedding. Hamsters have a strong sense of smell and the scent may be overwhelming for them. If the cage is kept clean and the bedding is frequently changed, there is no need for an odor retardant bedding.

Cat litter or cat litter like bedding products should not be used in your hamster's home. Dust and chemicals in the litter can create respiratory problems and neurological problems for your hamster. While commercial wood shavings are fine for bedding, do not use wood shavings from a lumberyard or wood shop. Often the wood has been chemically treated and is not finely enough processed for hamster cage bedding.

Shredded plain paper can be used as bedding, but newsprint or other heavily printed paper should not be used, as the ink can be toxic for your hamster.

Some hamster owners want to create an environment very similar to one that the hamster would have in the wild. While this is commendable, it is not very practical, and particularly if children are taking care of the hamster home. Bringing soil to the hamster cage so that the hamster can burrow and create tunnels can create an environment where there are fleas and other pests, unless the soil is sterilized. Changing out the soil is a big job, and not one that children can easily do. If you prefer a more natural environment, you can buy sterilized gardening soil or compost and add clean sand to it, but be aware that it may contain additives that could be harmful to your hamster. Keep in mind that a hamster that tunnels through soil or sand is going to be dirtier and create a bigger mess.

Another solution could be to build your hamster a separate sandbox that they can play in from time to time. As an example, you could fill a small heavy-plastic bin with clean sand and soil, and put it in your hamster's cage for a few hours at a time.

A Nest Box

Your hamster will want a separate shelter that is darker, cool, and comfortable for housing its nest. At the pet supply store, you can find a myriad of appropriate structures that will fit the bill for your hamster's nest box. The criteria for a structure is:

- The structure should be easily removable for cleaning by lifting it off the top of the nest. It will not need to be cleaned constantly, but it can begin to smell of urine and serve as a home for insects and mites if not cleaned occasionally.

- The structure should have an easy-access entrance, but not be so open that a lot of light can enter. Remember, the purpose of the nest box is so your hamster can be tucked away and have a darker, quieter sleeping space.

- The structure should be made of material that the hamster will not chew. Except for temporary use, cardboard is out. Hard plastic, pottery, and glass are good choices.

If you look around your house, you may find several safe, interesting structures to use as a nest room. Make sure the structure is small so that the hamster feels safe and snug in its nest, and so that the structure does not take up too much room in the cage. It is okay to put two nest structures in the cage, but only one is really needed.

Besides a nest structure, your hamster will enjoy other temporary structures where they can hide or run through as a short tunnel. A temporary hamster hideout can be made from an empty tissue box. Empty food cans with both ends removed and with no sharp or raw edges can be fun for them, as well as empty toilet paper or plastic wrap tubes, cylindrical oatmeal containers, or pieces of PVC pipe. If you have a chubby hamster, make sure the tube is wide enough for your hamster to get through without getting stuck.

Nest Building Material

Your hamster will build their nest inside the nest structure. All you need to do is provide nest-building material for them, since they obviously can't go out and gather it for themselves. Hamsters like to have a variety of nest-building material such as small scraps of cloth or ribbon, tissue paper that can easily be shredded, and bits of hay and grass (that has not been sprayed with pesticides and chemicals).

Syrian hamsters are industrious and make fast work of building their nest. Do not be surprised if your hamster does not get busy on the nest as soon as they find the nest-building materials you have put in their cage. Once started, the hamster will probably continue to work on the nest until it is completed, though they may add new material to it as they find it.

Once your hamster has built their nest and gotten it just the way they want it for maximum comfort, show them the respect they deserve and let the nest be. Don't try to add to it or change it, just let it be.

Water Bottle or Dish

Water bottles are preferable for the hamster cage over water dishes. Hamsters are silly creatures that like to frolic in their dishes, and they can make quite a wet mess with their water dish. If you are gone during the day, your hamster could empty their water dish without you knowing it and be stuck without water for several hours.

When it comes to hamster supplies, a water bottle is one thing where quality matters because your hamster needs fresh water available at all times to stay healthy. Choose a glass bottle or a heavy-duty plastic one that does not contain BPA. A stainless steel drinking spout is preferable. Choose a medium size water bottle that holds enough water for a couple of days, but wash the bottle and change the water daily. As a precaution, you may want to clip an extra small back-up bottle onto the cage, in case something malfunctions on the primary water bottle while you are away from home. The bottle should be clipped about five to six inches from the bottom of the cage so the hamster can reach the drinking tube when it stands.

When you wash the bottle, which should be done daily, use a tiny brush to get into the tube. Make sure you rinse away all soap residues.

If you choose a water dish over a water bottle, make sure it is a heavy dish that cannot be moved around by the hamster. The dish should be placed in a separate area at the perimeter of the cage instead of in the open area of the cage. Your hamster will probably fill the dish with bedding and may stand or play in the dish. If you choose a dish over a water bottle, it's important to keep the dish filled with water, and to monitor whether you hamster has become wet from playing in the dish. It cannot be stressed enough that a hamster with wet fur is susceptible to colds and diseases such as wet tail. Also monitor whether the dish has been turned over and made the bedding around it wet. Wet bedding is a breeding ground for harmful bacteria, and can make the cage smell bad.

Food Dish

Just like the water dish, the food dish should be heavy enough that the hamster cannot move it around, but short enough that the hamster can access its food without climbing into the dish, and when on all four legs. Small ceramic bowls or dipping bowls make great hamster food dishes, but no matter what you fill with food for your hamster, they will fill their cheek pouches and take the food to the spot where they want to store it. At a later time, they will forage for the food. So don't be shocked if you fill the food dish and it is quickly emptied.

For your hamster's enjoyment, sprinkle a few seeds or nuts outside of the food dish so they can hunt for their food.

© Petro Teslenko @ Fotolia

Hamster Toys

Happy hamsters are not idle creatures. They need stimulation and activity. Hamster toys can provide this. Put some thought into hamster toys before purchasing them or putting them in your hamster's cage. Are they sturdy and well-built for endurance and the type of activity they are intended for? Are they safe for your hamster when you are not there to watch him play?

Some toys are meant to be left inside the cage, and others are best used when you take the hamster out of the cage. Too many toys in the cage at once can make the cage seem crowded. Your hamster will tire of the toys in its cage, so put in just a few at a time and trade them out every few days. Trading out the toys gives you the opportunity to clean the toys and to examine them for cracks, breaks, rough edges or other problems that could hurt your hamster.

Hamster toys should be appropriate for the size of your hamster. Though it may be tempting to give your hamster small cat toys, it is usually not a good idea. Cat toys are not made for gnawing, nibbling animals such as hamsters. While puppy and small dog bones are made for chewing, dogs have the ability to digest the chewed bone, and hamsters do not. It is best to stick with toys made specifically for hamsters. You know they are safe for your tiny hamster.

The most popular hamster toy, and the object of so many hamster jokes and anecdotes, is the classic hamster wheel. The wheel provides excellent exercise for your hamster, but if the wheel is left in the cage, your hamster may actually become addicted to it and use it too much. If you keep the wheel outside of the cage and take the hamster out daily to run in it, you can control the amount of time your hamster spends in the wheel, as well as enjoy watching them play.

A hamster ball is an excellent toy for hamsters owned by young children. A parent can allow the child to hold the hamster for a few minutes, and then put the hamster in the ball for extended play time without the hamster escaping. It is important that young children understand that the ball can't be thrown like a regular ball!

There are variations of the hamster ball, including a hamster car that features the classic plastic ball in the middle as the car interior, and wheels on the front and back of the car frame. As the hamster runs in the ball, the car moves. Very cute!

Where Will You Place Your Hamster Home?

The outdoor world is too dangerous and uncomfortable for the pet hamster. They do not do well with temperature extremes, the hot sun beating down on them, or in very cold temperatures. Captive in a cage, hamsters would be sitting ducks for neighborhood cats and other animals. Hamster homes should be kept indoors, with hamsters being taken outdoors for fresh air and sunshine only when you take them out.

Since your hamster will choose to sleep a good deal of the day, it is best not to have their home in a high traffic area if you have a busy, active household. For the same reason, keep the cage in an area that is not brightly lit by artificial or natural sunshine during the day. Remember that the sun moves throughout the day and an area that is not sunny in the morning may be very sunny in the evening. Keep in mind that your furry friend's natural instinct is to cuddle into a soft nest that is underground where it is almost dark and cool.

If you want your hamster to enjoy an outside view, it is best that they enjoy it from a bit of a distance. Direct sunlight and cold drafts can impact the hamster if placed in front of a window. Hamster homes should not be placed near entry doors if you live in a cold climate, as they will be blasted with cold air when the door is opened. Avoid putting your hamster cage too near air conditioner or heater vents. Hamsters have adapted to human homes, and seem to prefer temperatures in the range of 65 to 80 degrees Fahrenheit. (The ideal temperature for newborn hamsters is 70-75 degrees F.) This does not mean that your hamster cannot survive temperatures a little lower or higher, but that you should strive for that range for your hamster habitat.

Particularly if you cage your hamster in a heavy glass aquarium, you want to set the cage on a sturdy, stable table or stand of some sort that will not topple over. The cage should not hang over the edges for someone to bump and accidentally knock over or hang their clothing on.

Hamsters are famous for chewing on electrical cords. Make sure you put your hamster home in a place where your hamster does not get the chance! Your hamster can be electrocuted if they chew on electrical cords. Do not under estimate the hamster's ability to reach and figure out clever ways to grab nearby electrical cords, computer cords, phone charger cords, or window blind cords from their cage. And speaking of window coverings, your hamster has pretty good taste in nesting material. If given the opportunity, they may decide to use curtains as nesting material. The same goes for clothes and other fabric that may be reachable from the hamster cage.

Never enclose your hamster cage in a closet, drawer, or cabinet where they do not have plenty of fresh air.

Put your hamster cage in a well-ventilated room that gets fresh air, and where they will not inhale toxic fumes. This includes fumes from chemical cleaning supplies, fertilizers and yard care products, and even strong cosmetic and personal hygiene products.

Have you heard the story of Molly? Molly, a young college student, adored hamsters and finally decided she had the time to care for one. She set up the hamster habitat just right. She carefully selected the cutest teddy bear hamster she could find, and took great care of the hamster…for the five days that it lived. Thinking that she must have bought a sickly hamster, Molly went to another pet store and selected another hamster. That hamster, more robust than the first, lived for almost two weeks. Molly was heartbroken when it died. She reviewed everything she was doing to take care of her hamster and could find no fault with what she was doing. She talked to the pet store employees and they confirmed that Molly was taking good care of her hamster. To help cheer up Molly, the pet store employer said that Molly must have gotten a hamster that was already sick, and insisted that she take another hamster home. He carefully handpicked a robust, healthy hamster for Molly. Just like the first hamster, the third hamster died within five days.

Molly was convinced that she was doing something wrong in her hamster care, but she could not figure it out. She re-read the hamster guide she had, and checked hamster books out of the library to read. Each book confirmed that she had been taking good care of her hamster, but Molly was too sad to get another hamster and risk it dying.

A few weeks later, a friend of Molly's from out of town came for an overnight visit. After a wonderful breakfast, Molly and her friend got ready to go out sightseeing. As Molly was finishing her hair, her friend walked into the bedroom and started gagging because of the hair spray that lingered in the air. "Are you trying to kill me with that hair spray?" Molly's friend asked.

When Molly's friend asked the question, Molly glanced over at the empty hamster cage that sat near her vanity table where she styled her hair once or twice a day. A light bulb came on in Molly's head! Molly looked at her friend and told her the pet store would be their last stop of the day.

Molly's story had a happy ending because she finally realized that the fumes from her hairspray were making her hamsters sick. After she got another hamster and moved the cage to another room, the hamster lived out its full lifespan.

Be very selective about where you park your hamster cage. Your hamster's life may depend on it!

Cleaning Your Hamster's Home

Even though your hamster is a clean creature, their house will need to be cleaned regularly by you. The best defense against sickness and disease is a clean, healthy environment. That means if you want your hamster to be healthy and happy, and of course you do, you need to clean their cage thoroughly no less than once a week, and preferably twice a week.

When you clean the cage, gently remove your hamster, first. Put it in a safe, secure place while you are cleaning. As a side note, it is never a good idea to let your hamster have the run of the house, particularly when you are not able to watch its every move. There are dozens of things that could go wrong and create injury or death for your hamster. Many hamsters have met their demise by innocently scampering across the floor to have an adult accidentally step on them or close a door on them. At the very least, your poor hamster will be stressed if it surprises someone and is blasted with a loud scream.

Okay, enough of a break—let's get back to cleaning the cage. In general, hamsters keep their nest clean and do not use their sleeping area as a bathroom, but this is not always the case, and it is likely to happen occasionally. With that in mind, when you clean the cage, lift the structure that covers the nest and gently lift the nest out of the cage so that it can be put back after you clean the cage. If you notice any odors emanating from the nest, it is time to toss the nest and let the hamster rebuild. There are special considerations for the nest when Mommy hamster is pregnant or nursing newborn pups. In a nutshell, the consideration is to leave the nest alone. There are more details about this in the chapter on hamster pregnancy.

Take out all of the hamster's toys and exercise equipment, water bottle or dish, and food dish. Toss the dishes and toys into a bucket of hot soapy water to soak while you are cleaning the cage. This will make clean up faster and easier.

Remove all of the bedding from the cage floor and dispose of it. Do not save any of the bedding to be added to clean bedding. Also, dispose of any food scraps you find in the cage. Hamsters are hoarders and you may not know how long the food has actually been in the cage or whether it is contaminated with hamster urine or droppings.

If your hamster house comes apart, disassemble it so you can clean in all the seams. Remove the lining tray, if there is one. Using a clean rag and mild disinfecting soap, thoroughly wash the entire cage from top to bottom, and inside and out. When you are done, rinse the cage thoroughly and make sure you don't leave behind any soap residues. Dry the cage thoroughly and let it air out for ten or fifteen minutes before putting in clean bedding.

Some find it easier to wash the bulky hamster cage outside, using a water hose to rinse it. If you do wash the cage outside, take a clean towel out to set the clean cage on so germs from the ground do not immediately contaminate it. If you wash the cage in the shower or in the kitchen sink, disinfect afterward.

Now that your hamster has a safe, clean home, let's figure out how and what to feed it.

© Mirko Raatz @ Fotolia

6: What Do Hamsters Eat?

Like most animals, hamsters like to eat, and a big part of their natural life is spent gathering food to ensure their survival. Never mind the fact that your hamster has you to fill their food dish; they still spend a good deal of time foraging for food, even though their foraging expeditions are quite limited in their cage.

Hamsters are omnivores, meaning they eat plants and animals. Your hamster has quite a varied diet, but there is one important thing to remember when feeding the hamster. Hamsters adapt easily to a particular kind of diet, and they do best if the diet is not drastically changed. In other words, if your hamster is used to a diet of seeds, nuts, fresh vegetables, and a little fruit, it might not fare well for a while if you suddenly switched to feeding it only pellet food, even though there would be nothing wrong with the pellet food. At the very least, the hamster would have an adjustment period where it might have some minor digestive distress. Therefore, it is best to decide ahead of time the type of diet your hamster will eat. You can continue to feed it the diet it was fed before you purchased it, or change the diet for the long term.

Hamster owners usually lean toward one of two types of diet for their hamster. Some stick almost exclusively to pre-packaged hamster kibbles because they believe this is the simplest way to ensure the hamster gets all of the necessary vitamins and minerals necessary to grow and develop properly, and stay in good health. Hamster kibbles, which come in compressed pellets and nuggets can provide complete nutrition for the hamster. For maximum hamster health, the pellets should consist of around 18% protein, 3% fat, 60% carbohydrates, .5% calcium, and a maximum of 8.5% crude fiber. It is best to purchase the pellets in small amounts at first. Sometimes hamsters do not like the pellets and will not eat them.

Other hamster owners like a more varied diet for their hamsters, and feed them many of the same raw and fresh foods they eat. It's best if hamsters are given a balanced diet of grains, nuts, seeds, fresh, raw vegetables and greens, raw fruit, and bits of clean protein such as eggs, fish, or cottage cheese.

Hamsters will eat just about any kind of food, but there are a few foods they should not consume. They should not consume sweet sticky foods that can stick in their cheek pouches. This includes foods such as raisins and candy. Taffy could be a hamsters worst food nightmare! Actually, according to Percy Parslow, author of *Hamsters* (T.F.H. Publications, 1995) pickles and alcohol are a hamsters worst food nightmare. He states that they will die if they eat pickles or consume alcohol. Whether this statement is true or not is yet to be determined.

Avoid giving your hamster cooked people food or food that is spicy, heavily salted, or high in sugar or chemicals. Hamsters may not like such strong-tasting foods, and for the same reasons that people do not do well on such foods, neither do hamsters. Do not feed fried foods or foods heavy in oil. Feeding citrus fruits such as oranges, lemons, grapefruit, and limes should be avoided. Do not feed your hamster frozen vegetables, uncooked dry beans, the green part of potatoes and tomatoes, or sprouting potatoes. Food for hamsters should not be hot or cold, but be at room temperature.

Feeding hamsters small, hard dog treats occasionally can help keep their teeth whittled down. Tossing a bit of high quality hay in the cage for the hamster to discover provides roughage.

Hamsters like eating insects. If you are so inclined, you can usually buy mealworms or insects such as small crickets or grasshoppers from pet stores. Be cautious about gathering insects from the wild for your hamster, as the insect may have been sprayed with insecticides or eaten plants that have been sprayed.

Hamsters should always have access to water, but if given consistent access to leafy greens and moist foods, the hamster will probably drink less water. Hamsters that eat mostly pellets are more likely to drink more water.

How Much Food Does my Syrian Hamster Need?

In general, Syrian golden hamsters, which are the larger hamsters, will consume about one-half ounce of dried food that includes grains and mixed seeds. The smaller Dwarf hamster will consume only about half that amount. In addition to the dried food, hamsters should also receive other foods to balance out their diet more completely. They like leafy green vegetables, broccoli, carrots, and fruit, except for citrus fruit, but the watery vegetables and fruit should only be fed in small amounts at one time. If a hamster eats a large portion of watery vegetables all at once, they may develop watery stools or diarrhea.

It is best to chop vegetables and fruit into small manageable chunks for your hamster. They will pick up the small chunks with their paws and nibble. If the chunks are too large, the hamster may not be able to pick it up, and they may become full before eating it, leaving it to decay in the cage and create odors.

When is the Best Time to Feed?

Since hamsters are creatures of habit and routine, it is best if you can feed your hamster at about the same time every day. About the time your hamster wakes up in the evening may be the perfect time for him to eat. This allows the well-rested, energetic hamster to sort and store its food. Hamsters need to be fed only one time each day. If, for some reason, you forget to feed your hamster before leaving for work or going away for several hours, no worries. You can rest assured that your hamster has a little stash or two from which to retrieve enough food to survive a missed feeding. However, do not get into the habit of missing feedings. Your hamster will quickly develop a routine of eating at a certain time each day, and may be stressed if there is little or no food.

Chew Sticks

Since hamster teeth keep growing for the span of their life, it is crucial to provide them with a way to naturally file down the teeth so they are not overgrown and interfere with the hamster's ability to eat. In the wild, hamsters gnaw on sticks, pinecones, and bark to whittle down their teeth. You can provide the same type of things for your caged hamster. If you are gathering any sticks from nature, be sure that they are free of anything that could harm your hamster.

At pet stores, you can purchase small wooden blocks, usually referred to as chew sticks, for your hamster to gnaw on. Why not go outdoors and pick up a few sticks? You can do this, but you need to make sure that there are no parasites living in the wood and that the wood has not been sprayed with any chemicals. You should not give your hamster cedar wood to chew on, as the cedar oil can create respiratory problems in hamsters.

Feeding your hamster a small, hard dog biscuit about once a week can also help keep manage their teeth. Check the ingredients for the dog biscuit before feeding, but generally hard dog biscuits are comprised of grains and vegetables and are safe for hamster consumption.

© Geza Farkas @ Fotolia

Here is a list of foods that are generally deemed safe food for your hamster.

Apple (with seeds removed)

Banana

Blackberries

Cherries (with pit removed)

Cranberries (fresh not sticky dried ones)

Grapes (seedless)

Honeydew Melon (not watermelon)

Peaches (pitted)

Plums (pitted)

Raspberries

Strawberries

Asparagus

Broccoli (in small amounts)

Cabbage (in small amounts)

Cauliflower

Carrots

Cucumbers

Spinach

Celery

Corn on cob (small pieces)

Bread

Cooked minced beef (only small bits, and make sure there is no fat)

Cooked poultry

Deli Ham (small bits only)

Cheese

Cottage cheese

Grasshoppers and crickets

Mealworms

Eggs (boiled or scrambled)

Dog biscuits (Check ingredients label)

Cooked plain brown rice

Nuts and seeds (no almonds)

Lentils

Bran and wheat germ (in small amounts)

Baby food (organic, without additives)

Unsweetened cereals

Dry toast

Oatmeal

Unsalted popcorn

Here is a list of foods that should not be fed to your hamster.

Buttercups (flower)

Chocolate (toxic)

Onion (toxic for some animals)

Garlic (toxic for some animals)

Peanut Butter (can get stuck in pouches)

Sandwich meats (contain preservatives and high salt)

Apple Seeds

Processed canned foods and other processed foods

Candy

Pie/pastries/cake and high sugar snacks

Pork

Potatoes (raw)

Kidney Beans

Eggplant

Avocado

Raw Rhubarb

Tomato leaves

Citrus fruits (including orange, tangerine, lemon, lime, grapefruit)

Watermelon

Fruit pits/ most fruit seeds

Jams

Sauces

Salt

Spices

Leeks

Scallions

Chives

Pickles

Mustard Greens

©ChrisArt @Fotolia

© The physicist @ Fotolia

7: Keep Your Hamster Safe

Just as any other pet does, your hamster depends on you to protect it and keep it safe. It is a big world out there for a tiny hamster. Though a caged hamster is usually safe from its natural enemies, it needs protection from human situations and living conditions, and sometimes from itself.

How to Safely Handle Your Hamster

When you first bring your new Syrian hamster home, it may not like you to hold it. It may squirm and wiggle, and try to escape. This may be particularly true if you bought the hamster at a pet store where it was rarely held.

If you are not handling the hamster correctly, it can bite you, escape and become lost, or fall to the floor and sustain injury or worse. Hamsters do not usually bite unless they are afraid. If your hamster bites you when you hold it, you know you have more work to do to help it feel secure and safe.

Your goal is to have a hamster that is calm, accustomed to being held, and relaxed when being held. This will make your hamster-holding experience much better, and keep your hamster safe. It will also keep your fingers from being bitten!

Allow your hamster a little time to settle into its new environment and calm down before you try to hold it too much. It will not take it more than a few days to realize that it is among friends! During the adjustment time, don't allow other pets, children, loud noises, or sudden gestures to disturb and frighten your hamster.

After your hamster has adjusted to its new home, you can start coaxing it toward your hand by putting your hand in the cage while holding a special treat, such as a few sunflower seeds or a honey-grain treat. Give the hamster ample time to sniff and move toward your hand, and do not push or force it. The hamster will learn the scent of your hand and get friendlier each time your hand brings it a treat.

After this adjustment period, you should start taking it out of the cage a few times each day. If you are not the only owner or caregiver of the hamster, let other owners and caregivers start holding the hamster, too. The hamster will develop an awareness of the smell associated with each person and his or her hands. He will associate this smell with trusted hands.

It is best to pick up your hamster after it has awakened from its daytime sleeping, and not while it is groggy and sleepy during the day. Hamsters like their routines and can be irritable when the sleep pattern is disrupted. Hamsters are busy about their business for several hours per day and need their sleep once they burrow into their nest.

The safest way to pick up a hamster is to cup both hands and gently slide them under each side of the hamster, and sort of scoop the hamster into them. With this method, the hamster doesn't feel any pressure from your hands. But it's also important that as you lift the hamster from the cage, you use one hand on top of the hamster's back to secure it, so it doesn't fall or jump.

If you consistently work on holding your hamster, both of you will adjust and find a system that works. If you happen to have a hamster that insists on biting, wear gloves and continue to work with it until it no longer bites.

Young children adore hamsters, but they must be instructed on safely and carefully holding them. Make sure the hamster has adjusted to its new habitat before introducing it to young children.

© Andy Lidstone @Fotolia

Keep Your Escape Artist Safe

If you talk to hamster owners, most of them have funny stories about how their hamster(s) escaped and where they finally found them. These sweet stories abound, and are fun to hear, but it is not fun when your hamster has escaped and you cannot find it! All you can think about are the many dangers that your tiny hamster could encounter.

Your escape artist is bound to get away occasionally, but you can minimize the escapes by making sure you take the time to tame your hamster so it does not bolt when you are holding it. Always make sure you calm the hamster as you take it out of the cage. Make sure you do not have any food or strong scents such as lotion on your hands, and let the hamster smell your hand first. When lifting or holding the hamster, do not make any sudden moves that would cause it to be frightened.

As soon as you realize your hamster is missing, take action. Restrain cats or dogs that might happen upon the hamster with less than pure intentions for the scared hamster. Close the lids on toilets, and close washer and dryer doors. If you have any plants that could be poisonous to your hamster in the event that it decided to nibble on it, cover the plant with a paper bag and put it up high.

Unplug cords that you can unplug and put insulated cord wrap on the ones that you must leave plugged in. Put away any open containers of any substance that could harm your hamster. This includes any packages of food that the hamster should not eat that have been left out on the kitchen counters.

Try to think of anything else in your house that could be a danger to your hamster.

Close all interior doors and entrance/exit doors. If your hamster is trapped inside the house, it is more likely that it will be recovered than if it gets outdoors. Closing doors blocks off more spaces for your hamster to go to hide. If all doors are already closed, it is less likely that someone will accidentally close a door on the missing hamster.

If there are teens or children in the house, there is a good chance that their bedroom floor might be partially covered with clothes or toys. Try to keep the floors as clear as possible to give the hamster fewer hiding places.

Some experienced hamster owners suggest setting a "trap" for your hamster, and luring them to the "trap" with special aromatic treats. One such trap is to put a few inches of bedding in the bottom of a few pails or other containers with tall sides that are about eight to ten inches tall, and set the pails in the center of each room in the house. Stack books or blocks, stair-step fashion, leading up to the rim of the pail, so the hamster can walk up the "stairs" to get to the treat, which you will set on top of the rim. The treat should be one that the hamster likes and be aromatic. A small chunk of apple or a bit of peanut butter on a sliver of cracker works well. The treat should be place so that when the hamster reaches for it, it falls over the rim and into the bedding in the pail.

Another possible way to locate your lost hamster is to utilize a trick shared by another hamster owner: tie long pieces of yarn around peanuts in the shell or other non-perishable treats, and leave them around the house on the floor and near some likely hiding places. If the hamster is hungry, it may go for the bait and drag around the food to try to get it to a safe place to eat it. It may even take the bait treat back to its cage to put in its storage pile of food.

It will be easier for you to spot the long, moving string than the blur of a scampering hamster. Also, if you make note of where you leave the bait treat, missing bait may help you discover where the hamster has been or where it may be going.

Some hamsters will go back to their cage because the cage is familiar to them. Leave the cage door open wide, and put some special treats in the cage.

Another trick to track down a lost hamster is to put flour or cornstarch on the floor in the areas where you think the hamster could be, and then follow the tiny little white tracks.

Where do hamsters hide? An escapee hamster probably feels scared and wants to find a quiet place that is dark and sheltered. Think about the places in your house that fit that description. Do not make the mistake of thinking any place is too small for your hamster to hide. When they burrow and hide, they can fit in amazingly small places. Hamsters can be very stealth, and can be very still, causing you to walk right by them and not see them.

Check all of the following places in your house:

70

- ✓ Under all furniture
- ✓ In dirty clothes hampers
- ✓ Behind stacks of books or magazines
- ✓ Behind drapes
- ✓ In closets
- ✓ Inside boots and shoes
- ✓ Under appliances
- ✓ In purses and backpacks
- ✓ In flower pots
- ✓ In cabinets in the kitchen and bathroom
- ✓ In dresser drawers that have been left open
- ✓ In toy boxes
- ✓ In any empty boxes or bags

If you are not able to locate your hamster, do not despair and give up completely. Hamsters can usually survive on their own for a while, and you never know when it may show up again. Hamster owners have been delighted to have their hamsters show up weeks or even months after they disappeared.

© Petro Teslenko @ Fotolia

8: Understanding Your Hamster's Body Language

Just for Fun!

Humans love giving their animals human attributes. There are videos that show dogs, cats, and hamsters "talking." Some of the cutest greeting cards, post cards, calendars, and photos feature pets dressed in human clothes, wearing sunglasses or hats, and doing things that humans would do.

There is great joy in giving voice to the furry creatures that do not have words to tell their owners how they feel. Of course, to some extent, you can only guess what they are really saying. But after years of observation by caring hamster owners, some expressions and body language is understood.

Below is a fun list of hamster actions that correspond with what your hamster may be saying to you. Is it completely scientific? No. Is it fun? Sure. The real point is that this chart reminds you to slow down and pay attention to your Syrian hamster. What is the point of having a hamster if you do not take the time to observe it and try to understand it? Take a look at the chart on the following page, and you'll never look at your hamster in quite the same way again

What Your Hamster Does	What Your Hamster Is Saying
Flinching	"That noise was really scary!"
Burrowing and collecting food, scampering about	"Woohoo! Life is good!"
Lies on back and bares teeth	"I'm really scared and I'll bite to protect myself if I have to."
Runs away when you pet it	"Enough with the petting already!"
Yawns	"It's time for my nap."
Growls	"I want to be left alone, now, please."
Acts irritated	"You are getting on my nerves. Back off and give me some space!"
Sitting up on haunches	"Wow, look at that! That's really interesting!"
Folds Ears	"I am paying attention!"
Creeps close to the ground	"I have no idea where I'm at. This is a strange place. I'd better lie low."
Puffing out cheeks	"Look at me! Aren't I intimidating!"
Leaping in the air	"I love my life. Today is a good day!"
Tail points up	"You are a revered hamster, and I'm shaking in my boots."
Hissing	"I feel threatened."
Chattering teeth	"I'm warning you..."
Squealing	"I'm ready when you are. Let's take it outside!"

© The physicist @ Fotolia

9: Hamster Health

For as small as they are, Syrian hamsters are sturdy animals that do not require frequent medical attention. Given a safe, healthy environment and an adequate diet, a hamster may live out its life span without a visit to the vet. Hamsters do not need to receive vaccines or visit the vet for checkups like most pets do. A hamster owner is capable of knowing when something is wrong with the hamster, if they make it a daily practice to observe their hamster and make note of any changes in the hamster's behavior, eating habits, droppings, or appearance.

Unfortunately, if a hamster does get sick and does not receive immediate medical attention, it can waste away very quickly. That is why it is important for you to know the symptoms of some common hamster ailments and what to do if you see the symptoms. Catching the symptoms immediately and taking action is crucial to your hamster's survival through disease and sickness.

Prevention of disease is always the best first line of defense. Do not get careless with cleaning your hamster's cage, protecting it from cold or extreme heat, providing a stress-free environment and a well-rounded diet.

Characteristics of a Healthy Hamster

For the sake of comparing a healthy hamster to one that might be sick, let us review the characteristics of a healthy hamster.

✓ A healthy hamster will have a soft, plush coat that is not matted, ruffled, or falling out in places. (It is normal for older hamsters of around a year old to start losing their hair.)

✓ A healthy hamster will have teeth that are yellowed and properly aligned. If the hamster's teeth are broken, and there is no evident explanation for the broken teeth, it can signal that disease is present in the hamster.

✓ A healthy hamster does not have a very wet or dripping nose.

✓ A healthy hamster does not have hazy or weepy eyes.

✓ A healthy hamster that is properly cared for has shiny, smooth skin under the fur. It does not have bumps and lumps or bites from mites.

✓ A healthy hamster is active during evening and early morning hours. A healthy hamster is not lethargic.

✓ A healthy hamster does not have stained fur underneath the tail.

✓ A healthy hamster has perky ears that stand up.

✓ A healthy hamster does not have a hunched over body.

✓ Healthy hamsters have a healthy appetite and don't refuse to eat. They are not excessively thirsty, but do drink water.

✓ Healthy hamsters do not have swollen abdomens.

✓ Healthy hamsters do not incessantly scratch their skin.

✓ Healthy hamsters to not suddenly develop an usual odor.

The Dreaded Wet Tail Disease

One of the most common and deadliest diseases among hamsters is the dreaded bacterial disease *proliferative ileitis,* commonly known as wet tail. The main symptom of wet tail is severe diarrhea. The disease is high contagious and can spread like wildfire.

How Does a Hamster Get Wet Tail?

The bacteria that causes wet tail is often present, but it is the hamster's environmental factors that allows the disease to cause the hamster to become sick. It is similar to humans that go to work at the office where bacterial or viral illnesses are going around. Some workers will get sick and others will not. The workers that are most likely to become sick are the ones who are stressed, have poor hygiene habits, have poor diet, have weakened immune systems, and so forth. Hamsters are vulnerable to wet tail if they live in dirty cages or overcrowded conditions, have a poor diet, or experience stress. The stress factor is the reason hamster may get wet tail when they first go to a new home, and is the reason that hamster owners need to make every effort to calm down their hamster and help it adjust to its new home.

Wet tail is a very serious disease and requires the attention of a veterinarian if you expect your hamster to survive the sickness. A vet will usually give an anti-biotic and anti-diarrheal medication for the disease, as well as prescribe fluid therapy to keep the hamster hydrated. While your hamster is ill, it should be separated from other hamsters. Special care should be given to keeping its cage clean and dry and making sure that the hamster stays warm and comfortable.

Deficiency Syndrome

When hamsters are not fed a varied diet that includes plenty of vegetables, protein, and carbohydrates, they do not get all of the vitamins and minerals they need. When this happens, they can become deficient in certain vitamins and minerals that are necessary for proper growth, development, and good health.

If your hamster starts losing its hair, has an overall dull appearance, and has a rash on its body, it could be suffering from deficiency syndrome.

Vitamin and mineral deficiency can be treated by changing the hamster's diet to include a variety of nutritious foods. If you have been feeding the hamster whatever you happen to have on hand, it might be a good idea to add a vitamin and mineral rich pre-mixed food to the diet and just supplement it with fresh vegetables and fruit.

Meningitis (LCM: Lymphocytic Chorio-Meningitis)

If your hamster lives in an area where there are wild mice running about, it may be at risk for meningitis. Meningitis is common among mice, but they can pass it on to young golden hamsters. It can transfer from hamster to people also. This form of meningitis should be watched for in particular if there are any pregnant women in your household, as pregnant women should not be exposed to the disease. It can cause premature birth and malformation of the baby.

Symptoms of the disease in the golden hamster can vary, but may include weight loss, and drowsiness. The growth of the hamster will also be slow and it may develop conjunctivitis (pink eye) and start to avoid light.

Mistakes That Can Make Your Hamster Sick

- Allowing your hamster to have contact with stray or sick animals can make them sick. Bacteria, worms, and viruses can be transmitted from other animals to hamsters.

- Unbalanced diet that doesn't include all of the vitamins, minerals, fiber, and protein that a hamster needs.

- Sudden temperature changes can stress your hamster and make it vulnerable to disease.

- Letting your hamster get wet and cold can put it at risk for sickness.

- Not allowing your hamster to sleep enough because his sleeping time is disrupted by loud noises or being picked up can eventually lead to sickness.

- If your hamster is not given hard dog biscuits or wood sticks to chew on, its teeth can create health problems.

- Soggy bedding in the cage puts your hamster at risk for diseases.

- If your hamster gets fleas or mites and they are not treated, your hamster is at risk for infections.

A Trip to the Vet

It's best not to wait until you need a veterinarian to find one. If you find one ahead of time, you will be ready to take your hamster to them when you need to. Also, if you've established a good relationship with your vet, they may be helpful in answering questions and giving you advice over the phone.

If you need to take your hamster to the vet, and it is not an emergency, try to take it in the late afternoon and evening hours after it wakes up from its sleeping time. If you take it when the hamster is drowsy, the vet might not get an accurate idea of what is going on.

When you take your hamster to the vet, take it in its cage. You may be tempted to change the bedding of the cage before you go, but don't. The vet may want to get a stool sample from the soiled bedding so he can test it for bacteria and such, and make a diagnosis.

Symptoms, Probable Cause, and Possible Remedy

(This chart is to be used for informational purposes only and is not to take the place of a professional veterinarian. Use the chart as a starting guide for what could be wrong with your hamster.)

HAMSTER BEHAVIOR OR SYMPTOM	PROBABLE DISEASE OR PROBLEM	POSSIBLE REMEDY
Sneezing, watery eyes, red feet, flaky skin, some possible hair loss, but still active	Allergies to certain foods, bedding, or household irritants such as cigarette smoke or cleaning chemicals	Change food and feed simple rice and veggies for a while. Remove household irritants
Runny nose and eyes, sneezing, lethargy	Common cold	Move cage out of drafty area, keep hamster warm. Feed a mixture of lukewarm milk and water mixed in equal parts, with a teaspoon of honey added. If no improvement in 2 days, take hamster to vet.
Severe diarrhea	*Proliferative ileitis*, commonly known as wet tail.	Take hamster to the vet. Vet will treat with antibiotics, anti-diarrheal meds, and fluid therapy.
Inflamed skin, scratching	Possibly parasites, poor habitat	Consult with vet for diagnosis and remedy
Refusing to eat	Injury to cheek pouch; improper	Call vet after food is refused for an entire

	temperature—too cold or too hot; problems with teeth	day
Bald spots in fur	Deficiencies in diet, old age	Evaluate diet and feed a complete diet comprised of carbs, fats, proteins
Limping or dragging one leg	Contusion or fracture	Call your vet for consultation
Labored breathing, sneezing	Pneumonia	Call vet
Light scratches or wounds	Fighting with other hamsters; snagged by wire or other sharp object in cage	Clean with iodine and watch for infection. Separate hamsters if fighting has occurred.

Hamsters and Old Age

Sadly, your hamster's lifespan is very short and it will reach old age in the blink of an eye. By then, you will have become very attached to the little furry friend, and it will be hard to watch it live out its last days. There is not much you can do about old age, except make your hamster as comfortable as possible.

Elderly hamsters spend a lot of time sleeping. They do not leave their nest unless they want to eat or to occasionally get a little exercise. They no longer scamper as they did when they were young. It takes effort for them to walk across their cage that once seemed so small when they were darting about it as a young hamster.

When a hamster gets old, it usually becomes much thinner. Sometimes they become blind as they age, but they can still use their sense of smell to get around.

Once your hamster shows signs of being old, its time alive will be very short. In most cases, it will go to sleep and not wake up again.

© heusler @Fotolia

10: Hamster Hygiene and Health

No matter how busy you get, you know that you cannot simply forego grooming and personal hygiene. You know this is an important, must-do part of your day. Personal hygiene keeps you healthy and ready to face the world. It helps prevent health and social ills.

And so it is with making sure that the hamster is able to stay clean, dry, and groomed as needed. A hamster's hygiene is directly related to its health.

If you are the parent of a young child who owns a hamster, it is critical that you put a system in place to be sure the child does not forget or neglect their hamster hygiene routine. Even the most responsible child hamster owners can tire of the routine or get busy and forget to clean the cage, provide dry bedding, or clear the cage of moldy, spoiled food. When neglected, all of these things can make the hamster very sick. Once a hamster is sick, without immediate medical care, and often even with medical care, the hamsters days are numbered. While it may be difficult for the parent to remind the child hamster owner of their constant responsibility for their hamster, it is even more difficult to watch a heartbroken child cry over their hamster that did not survive their neglect.

The hamster lives in a controlled environment that requires outside intervention from you. In other words, you control the level of care the hamster receives. While they truly need little assistance in actual grooming, they need very consistent assistance with the cleanliness of their environment.

Here is a checklist for careful and consistent care for your hamster:

✓ Without exception, keep your hamster's cage dry. Hamsters urinate and defecate in their cage causing unsanitary and wet conditions if left unchecked.

✓ Regularly check your hamster's nest. If there is an odor, it's time to toss the nest, provide more nesting material, and let your hamster start another nest. Over time, particularly if there are other pets in the house that may carry fleas or mites, the nest can be a harboring ground for unwanted pests. Fleas and mites can make your hamster miserable, at the least, and possibly make it sick.

✓ Check your hamsters paws and claws regularly. Are there any irregularities? Do you see any injuries? Is there anything lodged on the paw that could create discomfort or infection? Are the claws too long?

✓ Check your hamster's teeth. If they are moderately too long, you need to give the hamster wood chew sticks or hard small dog biscuits more often. If the teeth have grown too long, consult your vet about having the teeth trimmed or filed.

✓ Pay attention to your hamster's moods. Moods? Yes, hamsters have moods. To some degree, they can express how they feel by the way they act. For the most part, your hamster should be spunky and seem contented. It should scamper about and want to play. If the hamster seems sullen, irritable, or has lost interest in playing, it may mean it does not feel well or that something is amiss.

✓ It may seem a bit gross, but you need to pay attention to your hamster's bathroom habits. If your hamster suddenly stops urinating and pooping, it probably has a health issue that needs to be addressed right away. If the hamster's droppings become watery and runny, be on instant alert. (See the information in this book on wet tail.)

As shown in these photos, hamsters are wonderful holiday gifts for children and adults who already have everything…but a hamster!

© Anyka @Fotolia

© Puchikumo / Klara S @Fotolia

© Agodka @ Fotolia

© Photos by L @ Fotolia

11: Breeding Your Syrian Hamster

Some Syrian hamster owners find great satisfaction in breeding their hamsters for various reasons. Some breed the hamsters in order to pass along healthy, friendly hamsters to friends, family members, and others who want hamsters.

Those who are interested in exhibiting their hamsters in competition shows may want to breed to improve their stock and achieve the quality hamsters they desire for the competition.

If you wish to breed Syrian hamsters, there are several things to consider. First, it will cost you money. Even if you have all of the equipment and animals that you need, you should consider breeding a hobby, rather than a money-making venture. While hamster breeding may bring in a few dollars here and there, it is not a lucrative endeavor. Breeding large groups of hamsters can be very time-consuming and beyond the personal satisfaction of having bred and improved your stock, there is little other compensation.

If you don't plan on keeping the pups it is a good idea to secure somewhere for them to go prior to breeding, because once the process is started you are going to have a several tiny pups to deal with very soon. Remember that a golden hamster's gestation period is a short 16-18 days, and the gestation period for the dwarf hamster is only a few days longer at 19-22 days.

You will probably have plenty of people who will say they want one of the adorable pups when they are born, but people seem to back out on their wish when the time for them to take responsibility for the pup arrives! If you can find one source to take all of the pups at once, you will save a lot of time. When possible, line up a backup source, or two.

If you find a pet store that will take all or most of the pups from you, make sure they are serious about taking them as soon as they are ready to leave Mommy Hamster. Once the little guys start growing, they will each need their own cage and all of the other things that hamsters require. If you are able to sell the pups to the pet store, don't expect much money in return. Pet store owners have expenses, and they will need to make a profit off the pups to pay their overhead for housing and caring for the pups until they are sold to their customers.

How Do I Choose Which Hamsters to Breed?

After you have made the decision to breed hamsters, you will need to find suitable parents. The first step, of course, is to check for the sex of the hamster. The female is probably going to be the more critical choice for breeding. She needs to be old enough to breed successfully, but not old enough to create complications. The best age to initially breed the golden hamster female is at about eight to ten weeks. If she is any younger, she will still be maturing, and she may not be able to properly care for her newborn pups. It should be noted that there is a higher rate of cannibalism for hamster mommies that are too young. If the female is older, there can be complications, too. Female hamsters become infertile by the time they reach about a year old. As you can see, the timeframe that female hamsters can breed is relatively short, but they come into heat about every four to five days.

Though the focus may be on the female hamster for breeding, since she has the tendency to create potential problems, the male selection is also important. The male hamster should be about a month older than the female with which he is mating.

An important breeding consideration is the temperament of both hamsters. Evidence shows that a hamster that is docile and friendly will pass that trait along to its pups.

Hamster coat color and fur type can vary. There are four basic types for Syrians: short haired, long haired, satin, and rex. Colors are such as white, black, cream, and what is known as wild colored (strong color variations). All of these variations can be intertwined to create combinations.

The female should be in season after nightfall in the summertime. In the cooler months, she will come in later at night and for much shorter duration. She should be receptive every four days or so.

(C)usbfco @Fotolia

Introducing the Couple

Introducing the couples can be tricky, as the female will attack the male if she is not ready to mate. It's important to proceed with caution if the female does not seem cooperative. Some breeders say it is best to take the female to the male's cage because she is territorial and protective of her own cage. The female will instantly start to mark the male's cage with a secretion from her genitals, which has a unique smell during the time that the she is in heat. The male recognizes the scent as his signal to court the female hamster. Once he gets the go-ahead from his mate, he starts to lick her head and ears and stroke her lower buttocks.

As long as the female is receptive, the two hamsters will take a turn rolling over on its back while the other sniffs the genitals. The female may play a little game of hard-to-get by scampering away, but the male keeps up with her and eventually is able to nuzzle the female and push up her rear end. The female then stops and stands still so the male can mount her.

After the deed is done, the female relaxes and bats at the male. The hamsters will repeat the process until the female wants to stop. At that point, she will let the male know in no uncertain terms that the game is over. At this point, you should separate the hamsters to avoid a serious fight.

Other breeders say it is best to take the male to the female's cage because the female is more relaxed in her own cage. You may have to experiment with this to see what works best for you.

No matter which cage they are in, when given the proper stimuli, the female will strike the pose that indicates she is ready. The gesture is to put her tail up. If the female seems testy, it is a good idea to keep the female in a wire cage, and keep the male on the outside of the wire bars, until you know the female is receptive. If she is in the wire cage with the male on the other side of the bars, she will still be able to smell the male, but they won't be able to fight.

You can also rub the scent of the male on your hands and gently pet the female down her backside to gauge her reaction to the male's scent. If you get no response from her, she may not be ready. You can go ahead and try to put the male in with her, but you are risking a fight. If you know your hamster well, you will probably be able to notice her behavior changes that will let you know when she is ready.

When the hamsters do get together, they will mate several times, preening and cleaning between mating. Keep a close eye on the hamsters, as she will become aggressive and start to resist the male when she is done. Once she starts her aggressive behavior, it will be difficult to break up the fight.

If you are able to get the hamsters to successfully mate, you can expect hamster pups to be born in about 16 to 20 days for the golden hamster or 19 to 22 days for the dwarf hamster. (See the next chapter for care and information on the pregnant hamster.)

Helpful Breeding Tips

- ✓ Always find good homes for the pups before you breed. Don't count on people following through with their promise to take some of the pups, and have two or three backups. Sometimes students who are in 4-H club at schools want to raise hamsters for their 4-H projects. Sometimes elementary school teachers want hamsters for the classroom.

- ✓ Males and females of the same hamster litter are usually more tolerant of each other and can be caged together in a larger cage. However, this is not always true, and you should always proceed cautiously when putting any male and female in the same cage.

- ✓ Many breeders find it easier to breed Russian or cream-colored golden hamsters the first time they breed. These hamsters seem to get along better and have better temperaments.

✓ Males and females from different litters should not be caged together and should only be put together when it is time for them to mate.

✓ If hamsters are not healthy and their diet is poor, there can be problems with breeding. Some breeders recommend giving a small amount of wheat germ as a supplement to prepare hamsters for breeding.

✓ Females that are bred too young may not be able to produce enough milk for her litter of pups.

© yuliufu @ Fotolia

12: The Pregnant Syrian Hamster and Her Pups

Even though the gestation period for the hamster is short compared to most animals, waiting for the pups to arrive can keep you on your toes with excitement. Toward the end of Mommy Hamster's pregnancy, you will probably find yourself checking the nest daily, if not several times a day, for the pink pups.

You may be expecting to see a big change in your hamster's appearance throughout her pregnancy, but there will not be a significant change in the growth of her middle. Hamsters have short legs. If a pregnant hamster's middle became too large, they would not be able to move about without dragging their middle on the ground. However, you will notice some changes in your hamster's behavior once she is pregnant. You will see the mommy instincts for feeding her young kick in. Your hamster will start hoarding even more food than she did before.

Like any good mom, the pregnant hamster will also be about the business of preparing a safe place for her babies to be born and live for the first days of their life. She will scrounge around the cage for new nesting material and run back and forth, padding the nest. For this reason, you need to check the nest *before* you breed the hamster. Perhaps it is best to let the female hamster rebuild her nest several days before you breed her so the nest is fresh and clean for the new pups. Even so, she will still go through the ritual of padding the nest while she is pregnant, and you should provide plenty of interesting soft nest material for her to find.

Sometimes the pregnant hamster will decide she does not want to give birth to her pups in the existing nest structure, and she will find another spot in the cage to build another nest. Keep an extra structure that is a bit larger in the cage for this purpose.

Once the hamster is pregnant, do not disturb the nest at all, even for cleaning. Just do your best to remove all dirty bedding away from the nest. You can do this by sliding a sturdy, thin sheet of cardboard or metal up to the nest and lifting the dirty bedding away from the nest.

Two days before your hamster's delivery date, change the bedding in the cage for the last time before birth, even if you just changed it the day before. After that, do not disturb the bedding again until the first clean-up after the pups have left the nest.

Take Care of Mommy Hamster

After you have prepared the cage for pups, there is not much for you to do in regards to your pregnant hamster, except make sure that she is comfortable, has everything she needs in her diet, and is treated with extra gentle care. She is equipped by nature to take good care of herself and her unborn pups, as long as you properly take care of her environment.

Pregnant hamsters can be nervous and skittish. It is best to gently stroke them, but hold them less during their pregnancy. Don't allow young children or strangers to hold the pregnant hamster, as she may panic and bolt, and/or bite the person holding her.

Hamsters do not like loud noises at any time, but noise may be particularly frightful and irritating for a pregnant hamster. If you normally have your hamster cage in a busy area of the house, it may be a good idea to move it to a quieter area.

© Kryzsztof Bajor @Fotolia

The Pregnant Hamster's Diet

It is not a good idea, and there is no reason to significantly change a hamster's diet while she is pregnant, except to add extra protein. This can be done by adding extra bits of cottage cheese, nuts, hard-boiled eggs, and fish. As always, make sure she has a diet that is rich in vitamins and minerals, and that she is eating a proper combination of protein, carbohydrates, and fats. If you are concerned about your hamster's diet, consult with your veterinarian. The vet may recommend supplements during pregnancy, but most breeders agree supplements are not usually necessary.

The Birth of the Pups

The pregnant hamster likes her privacy when it is time for her to deliver her pups. Having an audience, no matter how quiet it is, can make her nervous. Leave the mommy alone when she goes to her nest to give birth. She will stay in the nest for several hours after the pups have arrived, but she should not be disturbed at all during that time, either.

It is crucial that you absolutely do not touch the pups once they are born. This can cause the mother hamster to eat her pups.

The birth can take place at any time, but it most commonly happens during the night. The hamster goes to her nest, sometimes several hours before the birth, squats, and waits for the first pup to emerge. She picks up the pup with her paws and takes on the role of delivery room doctor! With her teeth, she tears open the amniotic sac, then she eats the membrane and after-birth. She bites the umbilical cord. Her motherly instincts continue as she licks her pup clean. She repeats the process with each pup that is birthed. The average litter of pups is eight, though the litter can range from two up to around sixteen pups.

Hamster pups usually weigh about one-eighth of an ounce. They are born blind and naked. They are dependent on their mother to feed them and keep them alive. This means a good hamster mommy does not leave her pups hardly at all for the first few days after birth. Instead, she lies down on her side with her belly exposed and one leg up so her pups can quickly discover her teats and the source of their nutrition. The mother hamster usually has seven to eleven pairs of nipples to keep her pups fed. When the pups latch on to the nipples, they rub against the mommy hamster's body and this stimulates more milk production. If a hamster gives birth at too young of an age, she may not be able to produce enough milk for all of her pups.

The mother hamster is diligent about licking her pups during their first few days of life. The licking keeps the pups clean, but also helps them urinate and eliminate feces. Rather than let it contribute to a dirty, unsanitary nest, the mother hamster eats the tiny pup droppings.

While the mother hamster is nursing her pups, she keeps them warm by covering them with nesting material, so there is no need for you to try to keep the babies warm with a blanket or any such thing.

In the event that some of the pups are stillborn or die shortly after birth, the dead pups should be removed from the nest area. Only remove the pups when the mother is out of the nest. If she isn't leaving the nest at all, try to lure her out with a special treat that she really likes.

Do not reach into the nest area with your hands to retrieve the dead pups. If you can, find something in the cage, such as a couple of chew sticks, to use. Something from the nest will have the mother's scent on it already. If you cannot find anything in the cage to use, use a long-handled utensil such as metal tongs, and try not to disturb anything in the nest area.

The Ugly Facts about Cannibalism

When you think about breeding your hamsters, you have to be aware of and consider the fact that cannibalism can spoil an otherwise exciting hamster time. It can be very disheartening to wait for the birth of pups, only to find that your sweet mommy hamster has turned cannibal, and there are no pups. However, experienced breeders know that it is a common occurrence among hamsters and other small rodents.

The birthing of pups is quite incredible. Everything usually works perfectly as it should for a healthy mommy and pups, and all is well in hamster land. The mother hamster has built in instincts that help her do exactly what she needs to do, but sometimes something goes awry.

Sometimes there is simply no explanation for why a mommy hamster eats her pups. It just is what it is, and there is no way you could have prevented it. Sometimes there are logical reasons for cannibalism. If you are aware of some of the reasons for cannibalism, you may be able to prevent it in some cases.

Tips to Help Prevent Cannibalism

✓ Make sure the mommy hamster does not become agitated or upset while pregnant, during birth, or after birth. Keep the noise levels down. The pups are not out of the woods of cannibalism for several days after birth.

✓ Do not touch the pups until they have left the nest and are on their own.

✓ Do not change the bedding or anything else in the cage any later than two days before the birthing date.

✓ Pre- and post-birth, keep plenty of fresh food and nesting material in the cage so the mommy hamster does not feel stressed about providing for her pups.

✓ Don't breed female hamsters when they are younger than the recommended breeding start ages.

✓ Make sure the female hamster gets plenty of protein in her diet at all times, but especially during pregnancy.

© kontur-vid @Fotolia

© mhphotos @Fotolia

The Pups

When pups are born, they are not very cute for several days when they finally grow fur. They are born hairless and with their eyes closed. Newborn hamsters cannot hear. Their forelegs and back legs are very wobbly and not of much use for mobility upon birth. Since they cannot walk, the mother hamster picks up her pups with her teeth and transports them back to the nest if needed. Occasionally, a pup may latch on to the mother hamster's teat and take an unexpected ride outside of the cage with Mom. For this reason, you should check around the hamster cage each time you let your hamster out, especially if you have a cat or dog that might quickly feast on the baby hamster.

If the pups are smaller than usual, the mother hamster may put the pups in her cheek pouches to transport them if she needs to move them.

On the day of birth, the mother hamster will massage the pups' abdominal area to help them go to the bathroom. This doesn't hurt the pups at all, and is quite necessary. Mommy hamster licks her pups to clean them, and she nurses them, and keeps them warm. She knows just what to do to take care of her newborn pups!

By the second day, the pups have gone from pink skin to a dark skin. The pups continue to nurse, but around the fifth day the mommy hamster starts to bring bits of food to the nest for the pups to nibble on. It is also around the fifth day that the pups develop a thin coat of fine hair.

When the pups are about ten days old, they see the big wide world for the first time when their eyes open. It is about this time that the pups become adorable. Their puffy little cheeks are obvious, and they are able to fill and empty their cheek pouches. By this point, the pups can go the bathroom without help, and are getting very close to venturing out on their own.

Around the two-week mark, pups are playful and enjoy silly hamster games with their litter mates. This can be the greatest time to closely observe the hamsters if you are looking to be entertained by them. They scamper and play outside of the nest, and become braver each day.

When the pups are 21 days old, they become independent. In some cases, the mother hamster is relieved to be done with her duty and will start to become agitated with her bothersome pups if they hang around any longer. This is the time for the pups to say goodbye to their mother hamster's cage and go to their new homes to start a life of their own. This is also the time that male and female hamsters that do not get along should be separated. From this point, it will not be very long until the pups become the hamsters that are bred, and the cycle will start again. Thus is the life of the hamster!

©Vera Kuttelvaserova

©williecrossin @Fotolia

13: Syrian Hamster Tidbits

Likely, your hamster will bring you many hours of enjoyment as you observe it and play with it. You never know what a hamster will do next. It might sit quietly for several minutes, as though it is about to fall asleep, only to have a burst of energy and dash across the cage as though its tail is on fire. The unexpected is part of the charm of the charm of the hamster.

The more you know about your hamster, the better you two will get along. This chapter is about the odd and end, possibly unexpected, possibly silly or strange things that you might not know about hamsters. Enjoy!

Did You Know that Hamsters Can Go Dormant?

Hamsters do not hibernate in the true sense of the word, but did you know that they can go through a period of dormancy? If the room where your hamster resides goes below 65 degrees, there is a chance that your hamster could slow down and sleep a lot more than usual. If the temperature does not rise, the hamster may go into a dormant sleep until the temperature rises. Your hamster is not dying or sick if this happens. It is a natural process where the dormancy mechanism in the hamster is working.

If your hamster goes into a dormant sleep, bring some heat into the room to warm the air temperature. Do not put a heater close to the hamster, put it in warm water, or do anything else to cause the sudden shock of going from a low temperature to a high one. Over a period of an hour or so, heat the room temperature to around 75 degrees Fahrenheit.

For your hamster's comfort level, and possibly for their survival, it is best not to let it go dormant. In some cases, a hamster is not physically strong enough to make it through the dormant sleep and wake up again. It's best to keep the air temperature around your hamster at around 75 degrees Fahrenheit.

Did You Know that Your Hamster is Intelligent?

With all of their silly antics, you may think your hamster is all fun and no brains, but in fact, hamsters are relatively intelligent little creatures.

If you have watched your hamster at play and "work," you have probably noticed that it learns things rather quickly, and has the ability to remember and find where it left its food stashes. It also seems to be able to remember how to get through tunnels and structures to get where it wants to go in a hurry. Some of this behavior is instinctual, of course, but also requires a certain level of intelligence.

Many hamster owners train their hamsters to do certain tasks or tricks. They train the hamster by enticing them with a treat, giving them a certain signal to start a task or trick, and then giving the treat when the hamster completes the trick or task. It's questionable whether you can teach a hamster to roll over like Fido, but you may be able to teach your hamster simple tricks such as climbing over an obstacle on signal, or coming to you when you whistle.

Hamsters seem to learn best by repetition. If you want to teach your hamster a trick, repeat the same process many times, several times a day for several days.

Your hamster is also smart enough to recognize your smell and voice over that of others. It knows that you are its caretaker and that it can depend on you. Therefore, it may readily come to you when you approach it, and ignore strangers.

Did You Know... ?

- In the hamster world, male hamsters are called boars and female hamsters are called sows—the same as for pigs. And you already know that baby hamsters are called pups.

- Syrian hamsters are diggers. In their natural habitat, they quickly dig long tunnels and burrows. Some species have ear flaps that keep dirt from getting in their ears when they dig.

- Hamsters can catch colds from humans, and humans can catch colds from hamsters! If you have a cold, it is best not to play with your hamster until the cold is gone.

- Hamsters can get stressed out. When they are confronted with scary conditions, loud noises, or changes that they do not understand and cannot handle, it stresses their body and can make them sick. Wet tail disease, which is a serious and common problem for hamsters, is believed to be initiated by stress, including stress from the hamster getting wet and cold.

- Syrian hamsters are territorial and solitary animals. They prefer to live and be alone rather than with other hamsters, although they can be quite social with humans when they have been tamed and trust the people that take care of them.

- Golden hamsters have the shortest pregnancy (gestation period) of any known placental mammal. The pregnancy period for a golden hamster is only 16 days. Mommy hamsters can have as many as 20 pups in one litter, but she usually has a litter of between eight and ten pups.

- Syrian hamsters are used for research for alcoholism because, for their size, they have large livers.

- Now, Syrian hamsters come in many different colors and patterns, but originally, there were only gold-colored Syrian hamsters.

- There are hamster clubs and hamster social groups that meet for physical meetings and online. If you type "hamster clubs" or "hamster organizations" into your browser you can find groups that will let you network with other hamster owners. Being part of a hamster owners group can be very helpful for receiving and sharing hamster information. If you want to find out if there is a hamster group in your local area, check with local pet stores or leaders of groups such as 4-H.

- Hamsters can be "shown" at some prestigious hamster shows or at many state or county fairs. To show your hamster, it must meet certain criteria. Look for a local hamster group in your area for more information, or contact your local fair administrators for information.

©Friday @Fotolia

©Khmel @Fotolia

14: Quick Tip References

This guide provides all the information you need for taking care of your hamster and keeping it safe and healthy. For those times when you just need a quick answer, this chapter provides it!

Shopping for a Hamster

- ✓ Shop at reputable pet store or breeder
- ✓ Check out the environment
- ✓ Check the hamster health carefully
- ✓ Prepare habitat before you purchase hamster
- ✓ Provide safe ride home from pet store

Hamster Habitat

- ✓ House only one Syrian hamster in one cage
- ✓ Make sure the cage is large enough for the hamster to scamper about, and to have separate areas for eating, sleeping, and bathroom habits.
- ✓ Make sure cage is escape proof
- ✓ Line the cage bottom with safe bedding
- ✓ Provide nesting material
- ✓ Provide water bottle or water dish
- ✓ Provide structures or small boxes and other "hiding" places in cage
- ✓ Provide wood for chewing to whittle down teeth
- ✓ Clean cage weekly or more often if bedding becomes wet
- ✓ Take decaying fruit and veggies out of cage daily

Hamster Health

- ✓ Find a good vet before purchasing hamster
- ✓ Keep fresh water in cage at all times
- ✓ Feed daily, and preferably at same time each day
- ✓ Avoid too many raw, watery vegetables or fruits at the same time
- ✓ Avoid processed and high sugar and high salt foods
- ✓ Feed hard dog biscuits to keep teeth filed

✓ Brush longhaired Syrian hamster weekly with soft-bristled brush

✓ Do not bathe hamster with water

✓ Bathe hamster with sand if a cleaning is necessary

✓ Check hamster often for skin irritations, abrasions, bumps

✓ Pay attention to hamster's bathroom habits and call vet if diarrhea persists

✓ Check hamster for fleas

Hamster Breeding Information

First mating: At about 12-14 weeks

Oestrus cycle (when hamster can get pregnant: 4-5 days

Gestation period: 16 days (can be as long as 18, but it is rare)

Keep Good Health Records

Part of taking good care of your hamster is managing its health. Keeping good health records for your hamster can be helpful if veterinary care is needed. If you rush your hamster to the vet because it is very sick or injured, you might not be able to remember answers to the questions the vet may ask.

It's a good idea to write down when you got your hamster, when/if bred, any sickness, abnormalities, or changes in health or behavior.

Copy the chart on the next page and use it to keep all of your hamster health records in one place.

My Hamster's Health Records

DATE	BEHAVIOR/ILLNESS	NOTES

Hamsters and Medicine

In most cases, if your hamster needs medication, your vet will give it to the hamster in the form of a shot while the hamster is in his care. If this is possible, it is best. It can be very difficult to give medicine to a squirmy, uncooperative hamster. The old trick of putting medicine in the food does not usually work well with hamsters. Their keen sense of smell tells them that something is wrong with the food and they may not eat it. However, if you put the medicine in their favorite treat, they may not be able to resist and may take the treat and gobble it up so quickly that they don't realize they've just taken their medicine!

In some instances, you may be able to put the medicine in the drinking water where it is more diluted than in the food. On the other hand, this is tricky because you can't be sure the hamster is getting the full dose of medicine.

© Stockcity @Fotolia

CPSIA information can be obtained
at www.ICGtesting.com
Printed in the USA
BVHW082246120620
581252BV00006B/192